Escaping from
Behavioural Poverty in Uganda
The Role of Culture and Social Capital

John C. Munene
Shalom H. Schwartz
Grace M.Kibanja

FOUNTAIN PUBLISHERS
Kampala

Fountain Publishers Ltd
P.O.Box 488
Kampala
E-mail: fountain@starcom.co.ug
Website: www.fountainpublishers.co.ug

Distributed in Europe, North America and Australia by African Books Collective Ltd (ABC),
Unit 13, Kings Meadow, Ferry Hinksey Road, Oxford OX2 0DP, United Kingdom.
Tel: 44(0) 1865-726686, Fax:44(0)1865-793298.
E-mail: abc@africanbookscollective.com
Website: www.africanbookscollective.com

ISBN 9970-02-479-5

Cataloguing-in-Publication Data

Munene, John C.
Escaping from behavioural poverty in Uganda: The role of culture and social capital/John C.
Munene, Shalom H. Schwartz, Grace M. Kibanja. -
Kampala: Fountain, 2005
–p.–cm
Includes index and bibliography
ISBN 9970-02-479-5
1. Poverty – Uganda   I. Sschwartz, Shalom H.   II. Kibanja, Grace M.   III. Title

Contents

List of Tables

v

Case studies

Figures

Acknowledgements

The qualitative and quantitative data reported in this book was collected with the support of the fund from the Netherlands Israel Development Research Project 94 -12.2. We are therefore grateful to Mrs Miriam Bar-Lev and Mr H.J. Mastebroek the Coordinators of NIRP for facilitating this research that has produced a book with a unique approach to poverty research.

Special thanks go to the members of the 263 Community Based Associations from whom we learnt the information incorporated in this book. Special thanks go to Hajati Kalema of Twegombe Women's Association for her support and readiness to provide us with information any time we needed it; Hajati Kalema, we recognise your bridging characteristics. We also thank the many people especially the peasants who were not benefiting from any association but spared their valuable time to respond to our long interviews.

We are grateful to the staff of Fountain Publishers especially Ruth Spriggs for her patience, professional knowledge and guidance in the editing of this manuscript.

Special gratitude goes to our families and friends for their thoughtfulness and patience while we kept away on our laptops and spent long hours day and night working on this piece. Our sincere gratitude to you all.

The Authors

Prof. John C. Munene is a Professor of Organisational Psychology at Makerere University. He has researched in the area of culture for over ten years while in England and Nigeria where he also consulted with organisations on cultural problems in productivity. He recently led a team that examined the impact of the defunct Nile power project on the cultural properties including spirits in Uganda. He published a paper with colleagues on the cultural dimensions of decision-making in African organisations. He has ongoing research in the area of social capital where he is currently examining the influence of social capital on the management of Universal Primary Education (UPE) in Uganda sponsored by OSSREA. He has edited three books and published several articles on the concepts of culture and social capital in several international journals.

Prof. Shalom H. Schwartz is the Leon and Clara Sznajderman Emeritus Professor of Psychology at the Hebrew University of Jerusalem. He is current President of the International Association for Cross-Cultural Psychology. He taught sociology at the University of Wisconsin-Madison for 12 years. He has developed theories of values at the individual level and at the cultural level and instruments to measure them that have been used in over 70 countries around the world. His current research examines individual differences in value priorities, values as determinants of socially significant attitudes and behaviour, value socialisation and development, dimensions of cultural difference and their implications, social structural and cultural explanations of national differences in value orientations.

Grace Milly Kibanja is a lecturer in the Institute of Psychology, Makerere University. She is currently pursuing a PhD in Social Psychology at the same university. Her current research is in the areas of Cultural Values, Gender, Negotiations, and participatory development.

Preface

This book examines the Ugandan experience of poverty from a Social Psychological Perspective. It focuses on the individual's behaviour as having a major role to play in making the individual poor, leaving him/her in poverty or helping him/her escape poverty. In this book, we introduce the concept of poverty carriers. Over the years, researchers have been focusing on poverty indicators rather than poverty carriers. As opposed to poverty indicators, poverty carriers are those activities performed by the individual, the acts that perpetuate or produce poverty, acts that must change if individuals are to escape poverty. Acts such as selling one's land, labour or one's children's labour are poverty carriers. We thus make the individual-in-poverty our focus of analysis in relation to the social, political, and economic structures that surround him/her.

We introduce the social psychological individual in order to emphasise the need to understand how the poor interact continuously with others, creating bonds and bridges to ensure their survival. We examine the role of culture in development by identifying and measuring cultural interfaces. We define cultural interface as an ongoing process characterising the way the parties (agents) relate to each other. We specifically distinguish between positive and negative cultural interfaces. A positive cultural interface occurs when people from groups that have complementary and compatible expectations or behavioural patterns come into contact; and a negative cultural interface results from the meeting of people with conflicting or incompatible behavioural patterns.

We then suggest social capital as a vehicle for moving out of poverty. We conceptualise social capital as the sharing by members of a community of a set of cognitions (beliefs, values, attitudes, expectations and knowledge) which they intentionally sustain through structures such as roles, rules, and networks. These shared cognitions motivate members to cooperate in joint pursuits and enable them better to predict one another's behaviour.

We also show how networking promotes people-centered participation in development. We distinguish between system maintaining and system transforming participation by referring to the many development policies in Africa that have failed to have impact simply because they embrace system-maintaining participation.

Finally we bring the social psychological individual upfront as the key player in determining his/her livelihood. Actions done by the individual or to the individual can affect the entire community positively or negatively. Using an example of seven districts in Uganda, we clearly portray the role of the individual in development.

1
Introduction:
An Overview of Poverty in Africa

In this book we examine the Ugandan experience of poverty using gendered eyes and focusing on the individual experience of poverty. Gendered eyes are necessary because women in Uganda experience poverty disproportionately. The focus on the individual is essential because, as we will show later in the book, the individual poor has rarely been considered. Focus has tended to be on structures including policies and institutions. Little is known of behavioural poverty or of what the individual does to become poor, to remain or sink deeper into poverty or to emerge out of poverty into well-being. This research adds to the growing literature that is beginning to address this gap (see UPPAP, 2000 and Sen, 1997, for instance).

There are two common ways to define poverty. Poverty may refer to lacking the resources to rise above a specific poverty line. This is called absolute poverty. The second definition refers to relative poverty, lacking the resources enjoyed by the average person in the society in which they live. Absolute poverty entails a level of income that imposes serious physical discomfort and suffering through hunger and disease and that prevents children and adults from reaching their full physical and mental potential. Malnutrition is the most acute physical expression of absolute poverty, imprinting itself on human flesh and bone.

Relative poverty is the mental suffering that derives from perceived inequity. It entails preoccupation and even obsession with thoughts about inequity, thoughts that prevent one from enjoying life. Relative poverty is a function of expectations. For instance, unemployed members of the elite feel deprived when they compare themselves with the employed. Harrison (1982) warns that the model of growth pursued by most third world countries has increased such inequity by channelling development opportunities to the already privileged, thereby marginalising the underprivileged and eliciting feelings of relative poverty.

In this chapter we present statistical evidence of poverty in Africa. We introduce the concept of the individual-in-poverty. This individual will be our focus of analysis and study in the work we report. We also deal with the contexts within which this individual operates, such as structures, institutions, and policies. We start with the individual, however, because a lot more has been written about the context of poverty than about the individual who experiences poverty. In order to focus on the individual poor, we define the individual in qualitative terms. This chapter describes the objectives, theoretical framework and methodologies used in the empirical study. Finally, we outline the various chapters that present and discuss the research we carried out.

Poverty in Africa: Statistical evidence that obscures the individual poor

The usual measures of poverty seek to describe its intensity (i.e. the depth and severity of life conditions), its scale (the number or proportion of people living in poverty), and the difficulty of eradicating poverty. Ali (1999) presents a recent picture of poverty in Africa, using various measures of the first two aspects. The proportion of the population below the poverty line, also known as the head count, indicates the scale or spread of poverty. The poverty-gap ratio shows the average gap or the range between individuals who are at the poverty line or below it. The gap is a description of the depth of poverty. The squared poverty gap ratio describes the rate at which poverty increases the further one moves down the poverty line. It measures the intensity or severity of poverty (Ali, 1999). Table 1.1 below shows Ali's findings for a sample of 20 African countries. The poverty lines listed are approximations of the absolute poverty level that differs somewhat across regions. In North Africa, absolute poverty begins at $60 per month or $2 dollars per day, in sub-Saharan Africa at $34 per month or $1.10 per day.

Table 1.1: Poverty in a sample of African countries

Region of Africa	Poverty line ($)	Head count ratio (%)	Poverty gap ratio (%)	Squared poverty gap ratio (%)	Gini coefficient	Mean expenditure ($)	Mean expenditure by poor ($)
Northern	60	20	5	2	37	135	46
Sub-Saharan	34	49	22	12	47	56	20
All countries	39	44	18	10	45	72	25

Source: Ali (1999, p. 88)
Note: We have rounded-off all figures except those in column 1.

Table 1.1 shows that 20% of the population in Northern Africa is below the poverty line, 49% in sub-Saharan Africa, and 44% in the twenty African countries surveyed. The difference, in terms of their expenditure, among the poor of Northern Africa, sub-Saharan Africa, and the 20 African countries surveyed is 5%, 22% and 18% respectively. The rate at which poverty increases among the poor surveyed also shows that the increase is steeper in sub-Saharan Africa (12%) than in Northern Africa (2%) and the sample of the other 20 African countries surveyed (10%).

These statistics indicate that poverty is five times as deep and 12 times as severe in sub-Saharan Africa when compared to Northern Africa. The last two columns of the table show that all Northern Africans spend on average $135 a month as against $56 for those living in sub-Saharan Africa. Similarly, the poor in Northern Africa spend $46 a month while the poor in sub-Saharan Africa spend $20.

The column marked 'Gini coefficient' presents another way of looking at poverty. It measures the distribution of income among the population in a country. For this statistic, the higher the score the more uneven the distribution. As the coefficients reveal, the income distribution is more unequal in sub-Saharan Africa than in Northern Africa. Ali (1999) has provided more specific data on income distributions in African countries.

Egypt and Ghana have the most equitable distributions, though, even in Egypt, the upper 20% of the population receives 20% of the national income. South Africa, Kenya, and Zimbabwe, in that order, have the least equitable distributions. Okwi and Kaija (2000) provide Gini coefficients for Uganda. Kampala City has the least inequitable distribution (Gini = 41), followed by the Central (43), Western (51), Northern (54), and Eastern (57) regions.

Quantitative analyses of national poverty, like those above, provide an overall picture and are useful for developing policies at the macro level. In Uganda, such analyses have demonstrated that rural Ugandans are poorer than urban, that poverty is more widespread in large households, that female-headed households are no poorer than male-headed households, that education is associated with improved welfare, and that there is high inequality in welfare distribution (Okwi & Kaija, 2000). However, the poverty statistics and the conclusions to which they lead fail to bring the individual who is poor into focus. A clear understanding of this individual is needed in order for policies, including macro-economic policies, to become cost effective. Ali (1999), reflecting on his own findings, arrived at a similar conclusion. However, he recommended a return to the development debate, which rarely ever considers the individual, in order to clarify what policies are required (see below and Chapter 5 for brief summaries of this debate). The Ugandan government and its partner NGOs have taken initial steps toward understanding the life of poor individuals by spending time with and learning from them (e.g. Learning from the Poor, (MFPED, 2000)).

Bringing the individual into the picture

The study that forms the basis of this book started with a similar aim of learning from the poor nine years ago. The goal was to study the individual-in-development, the individual trying to escape poverty. Then as now the objects of our study were and are the goal-directed individuals who go about their daily lives purposefully. We ask: how do they behave in reference to their kin, friends, foes, and others with whom they interact or expect to interact in the future. We call these persons 'social psychological individuals'. They are the most ignored unit in the study of poverty and development.

In psychological literature, Vygotsky's (1978) work most clearly articulates this view of the individual. The individual learns to master the environment by interacting with others. From observing others, the individual learns new ways of living more effectively than before. This new learning becomes part of the individual's repertoire of skills. Some or all of this repertoire becomes obsolete over time and in the face of new challenges. Hence, the individual must continually seek resources from the outside, typically from the cultural environment. With the aid of this cultural environment, the individual improves his or her mental functioning and is more capable of solving the new problems.

Our focus is on the poor. Therefore, throughout this book, we examine the social psychological individual who is trying to escape poverty. We seek to identify the people with whom poverty-stricken individuals must interact in order to promote their goals and the culture they may draw upon to improve their skills and mental capacity. We study individuals in terms of the actions they perform. In order for us as social scientists to be a useful part of the cultural environment upon which individuals in poverty can draw, we need to clarify which of the actions help them to escape poverty and which are futile or even harmful. Two theories are especially useful for this. The social capital model of development (Putnam, 1993) describes successful individuals as networking, trusting individuals who volunteer to help their neighbours and community with the expectation of long-term reciprocal benefit. The theories of basic human values (Schwartz, 1992, 1997) describe such individuals as persons who emphasise universalistic and openness values and seek to promote an egalitarian society. This study applies both these models as helpful for understanding the role poverty-stricken individuals play in either perpetuating or escaping their condition.

The approach we adopt may appear to blame the individuals for their own misfortunes. Blaming the poor is problematic especially in Africa where, too often, predatory state regimes, leaders and their extended families have governed and plundered African states (Bret, 1989, 1992). We do not intend to allocate blame. Rather, we wish to understand what the individual poor people do in their daily lives, what--from their own point of view–are the forces they face and how they respond to these forces. This objective has also largely dictated the central role that qualitative methodology plays in this book. Such methodology is needed to enter into the world of the poverty-stricken individual. Although we have committed ourselves to exploring the problem of poverty from a qualitative point of view, the study we report on used quantitative as well as qualitative approaches. We adopt this dual approach because quantitative information can describe and explain what is happening from an outsider's viewpoint, while qualitative information can explicate the why and the how from the viewpoint of the actors. We need both types of information especially about the poor and behavioural poverty.

Poverty: A qualitative view

We consider three perspectives used in the literature on poverty. It is not our intention to launch into a full debate on development theory. Rather, we will discuss development policies only insofar as they have been implemented in order to alleviate poverty. Table 1.2 summarises our discussion of common perspectives on poverty.

The first relevant perspective is the administrative. It views the poor as a group of people who fit an administrative category such as those falling below the poverty line (Ali, 1999) or consuming less than a certain number of calories per day (Cooksey, 1994). This perspective focuses on describing the material conditions of the poor. Okwi and Kaija's (2000) discussion of welfare distribution in Uganda is typical. It distinguishes between the well-to-do and the poor by describing typical household characteristics such as sources of drinking water, lighting, and fuel. The Ugandan poor, for instance, draw water from unprotected water sources, use *tadooba*[1] as a means of lighting their houses, and firewood as fuel. When the poor are defined administratively, the tendency has been to describe their squalor, debilitation, and humiliation (Sandbrook, 1982). Such descriptions shed little light on the processes that cause the poor to be located in the various administrative categories.

One consequence of the administrative perspective for policy is that it promotes approaches to development that emphasise relief or cost-sharing, basic human needs, and welfare action rather than capacity building or empowerment. Descriptions of the state of poverty are attractive because they are amenable to quantification and to increasingly sophisticated mathematical and econometric manipulation (see Ali, 1999). They point to the nature and quantity of suffering, but they leave a crucial gap in knowledge of the processes that lead to poverty. Models built on this perspective have dominated approaches to poverty alleviation in Africa. For forty years, however, these models have failed to provide solutions and, in some cases, have exacerbated the original poverty problem (McNamara, 1972; quoted by Sandbrook, 1982; Afonja & Aina, 1995).

Table 1.2: Three common perspectives on poverty and their implications for development policy

Perspectives	Typical indicators	Policy orientation	Development focus	
			Growth	People
Poverty as an administrative category	Conditions of the poor (e.g. calorie consumption)	Relief and cost sharing Redistribut-ion	Basic human needs	Welfare action
Poverty as a set of personal attributes of individuals or groups	Conditions of the poor (e.g. unemployment)	Capacity-building	Human capital development	Develop human resources
Poverty as a series of actions	Critical poverty-carrier activities by the poor	Transformation of resource values, covenants and institutions	Empowerment through organisation and control	

A good example of policy derived from the administrative approach is the Basic Needs model popular in the 1970s and 1980s. This model of development was proposed in order to overcome the failure to redistribute the wealth that had been accumulated in the African success story states of Nigeria, Kenya, Ivory Coast, and Malawi in the sixties and seventies (Sandbrook, 1982). The model was based on three principles: redistribute income to create demand for goods and services; uproot old economic activities through appropriate technology transfer; provide equitable access to public services such as education and health. By the mid-eighties, it was clear that the Basic Needs policy, like its predecessors, had widened rather than reduced inequalities (Sen, 1985). This policy failed despite good intentions and despite the lessons learned from the development policies and programmes that preceded it. We see such failure as intrinsic to the administrative approach.

A second perspective views poverty in terms of the problematic personal attributes of the poor, their state of being. These attributes make a community, a household, or an individual vulnerable (MFPED, 2000). The Women in Development movement in Africa is foremost in identifying personal characteristics of the poor (especially women). The poor are illiterate, unemployed or unemployable, have a high fertility rate, are ignorant of modern contraceptive methods (Afonja & Aina, 1995), and are legally defined as minors (Snyder, 2000). Other characteristics of the poor include polygamy, geographical and social isolation, and large numbers of orphans.

By focusing on the attributes of the poor, this perspective highlights the knowledge and skills they lack but which they need to compete successfully in the market economy. Policy recommendations from this perspective tend to emphasise capacity-building especially by involving the target population of the poor in decision-making. Change agents, including governments and donor agencies, have initiated and implemented policies that focus on human capital (people's own potential) in order to develop their resources. Various African universities have established academic departments that focus on women and on gender problems that prevent women from reaching or exercising their potential. A popular non-governmental (NGO) activity is adult education aimed at rural women. However, this model has also failed to deliver the African poor from poverty (Afonja & Aina, 1995). Korten (1992) suggests that its weakness is the inability to involve the poor fully in their projects, especially in the phase of programme design. Typically, the poor are expected to implement ideas that were developed by others.

A third perspective, informed by the social capital model of development, sees poverty as a series of critical poverty generating activities we henceforth refer to as poverty carriers. Social capital is the capacity of individuals to draw on others in case of need and the capacity of communities to offer help. It focuses on the actions that communities, individuals, and households undertake that may or may not perpetuate poverty. Examples are selling one's land, taking a loan, or marrying a second wife. The emphasis on what the poor do or do not do is a radical departure from the previous perspectives.

Working within this perspective, Korten (1992: 67) defined development as a process by which the members of a society increase their personal and institutional capacities to mobilise and manage resources to produce sustainable and justly distributed improvements in their quality of life consistent with their own aspirations. The poor members of society are those who are unable in any way to increase their capacities. Action, in this context, refers to participation including cost-sharing, decision-making, and empowerment. Through cost-sharing, the poor might increase the efficiency of development projects. Through decision-making, they might improve the effectiveness of the project and enhance their own capacity (capacity-building). If empowered, the poor could initiate development activities themselves. When people initiate activities they perceive will solve their problems, they make positive and sustainable qualitative changes in their lives (Paul, 1990).

The emergence of the action perspective was made possible by the popularisation of participatory research tools such as focus group discussion, mapping, Venn diagramming, gender analysis, and wealth ranking. The perspective also relies heavily on primary rather than secondary data. Its policy focus is on transforming the value systems and regulations by which people live. The gender equity campaign in Uganda and elsewhere in Africa exemplifies such policy. It seeks to change laws and other institutions that prevent women from performing activities that would allow them to reach their full potential. From the above it follows that helping the poor requires focusing on what they do–their actions, rather than their attributes or status–and the outcomes of what they do. The Ugandan Ministry of Finance and Economic Planning (MFEP) carried out a study of the poor adopting such a framework. We review some of its findings later in the book. An earlier Ugandan study that used the action model was a study of Primary Health Care (Munene, et al, 1997). We also used the action framework in examining how to improve the quality of Primary Education in Uganda. See below for a brief summary of this work.

We conclude that the administrative and personal attributes models of poverty, although most popular, are ill suited to help change agents to diagnose the fundamental problems that handicap the poor. Such problems are grounded in the activities that the poor do or do not initiate, activities that are informed by their value systems and prevailing institutional arrangements.

A key point we have stressed in this section is that the definitions of poverty and of the poor one adopts have crucial implications for the policies that change agents choose to set in motion. The following example of the action perspective shows the radical difference between studying primary data that reveal what people do and the everyday processes they experience (process data) and studying secondary data that point to the end results or outcomes of the actions of people we study (outcome data).

The Improving Educational Quality (IEQ) Project

The United States Agency for International Development (USAID), in collaboration with the Ugandan government, undertook to improve the quality of teaching and learning in primary education in Uganda. Among their activities was equipping primary schools with the instructional material, textbooks and syllabuses they required. Others included improving the management of primary education, training primary teachers (Teacher Development and Management System), and constructing new primary schools in areas where they would be accessible to a larger population of primary school-going age. Munene formed a team to evaluate the project which decided to collect process as well as outcome data. The team employed participatory learning and analysis methods to assess what was actually done by teachers, pupils, head-teachers, school management committees, parents and communities. Unexpectedly, the number of books available in the schools did not relate to school performance as indicated by the number and quality of grades. Rather, school performance depended on a set of specific teacher and pupil practices. The Improving Education Quality Research (Uganda IEQ Core Team, 1999; Munene et al, 1997; Carasco, Munene, Kasente, & Odada, 1996) isolated the following good teacher practices as enhancing the use of textbooks and improving school performance:

- Writing lesson objectives for the classroom periods in a way that enabled the teacher to measure whether or not the objectives were achieved.
- Selecting and preparing learning materials to reflect lesson objectives.
- Selecting and using teaching methods that physically engaged students in the achievement of lesson objectives.
- Controlling the class in order to achieve lesson objectives within the available time.
- Designing and implementing a classroom seating arrangement that helped all students to attain lesson objectives.

The specific pupil practices identified in the research as contributing to learning included:
- Going to school daily and working hard at writing and reading.
- Keeping one's exercise books in good condition and reading all the lessons.
- Playing good games, keeping good hygiene, and looking smart.
- Being disciplined and attentive in class.
- Avoiding such actions as smoking, having sex, abusing teachers and the community on the way to and from school.

The evaluation also identified poor teaching behaviours, such as:
- Relying on personal knowledge, particularly study notes made during teacher training.
- Borrowing teaching notes from other teachers.
- Giving half-dose to pupils (deliberately teaching less than what the curriculum called for).
- Spending time in activities that generate personal income in order to supplement salary.
- Directing and pacing teaching in large classes only for the pupils who understand.

Until recently, these concrete, qualitative findings were not available to those interested in improving primary education in Uganda. They shift attention away from secondary data, such as numbers of pupils who pass in each grade, to what actually takes place in classrooms. They provide clear guidance regarding what needs to be changed in order to improve learning in schools. They also make it easier to develop valid and appropriate theories to account for why and how some pupils pass while others fail.

The action perspective

Until recently, decision-makers did not have available to them this kind of concrete and detailed analysis of what the poor do. The lack of such information partly explains why the succession of policies and the many projects they spawned have largely failed to improve the lot of the poor in Africa. We do not claim that macro-economic and political economy analyses are unimportant. Of course, they play a necessary role in providing the broad picture in the fight against poverty in Africa. In our view, however, successful alleviation of poverty is more likely to come from a detailed understanding of how individual actions give rise to the statistics that macro-analyses uncover. It is worth pursuing this approach now because it has not been tried in the 40 years since African nations became independent.

In this study, we take for granted that the macro-economic figures on poverty are discouraging and that the social structures in which the poor carry out their daily business often harm them. We focus on what the poor can do to improve their economic situation, given the environment. We also consider, to some extent, the actions of those who design structures and policies that are hostile to the poor. In effect, we seek to spell out the concrete behavioural dimensions of development and escape from poverty.[2]

What we report is part of a study that culminated in exploring and examining, from the beneficiaries' point of view, specific, detailed elements of various development projects sponsored by Northern Non-Government Organisations (NNGOs) as well as by the Ugandan Government in collaboration with NNGOs. Our interest in development projects is from two angles. First donor governments increasingly channel funds through NGOs in order to deal with their own bureaucracies (Wallace, Crowther, & Sheppard, 1997). Second, NNGOs are said to have comparative advantages over alternatives such as the private sector and government departments. They are seen to respond to the needs of the poorest, they are people-oriented and work with people, they are empathetic in their approach to stakeholders / beneficiaries, they employ participatory development approaches and they conscientise Europeans (European Commission, 1995).[3]

The study in this book is, in effect, an examination of the relationship between cultural values and development in Uganda. It had the following objectives:

- To identify aspects of the Ugandan cultural value profile as distinct from profiles of nations around the world.
- To identify and compare value profiles of the major Ugandan ethnic/regional groups.
- To examine whether and how value priorities relate to socio-economic development in Uganda by comparing values profiles in more and less economically developed districts.
- To analyse the link between and possible causal influence of individual differences in values to the evaluations of features of specific development projects, to participation or non-participation in projects, and to levels of success in the projects.
- To examine which features of projects contribute to their attractiveness and success.
- To analyse social capital and its influence on the success or failure of the development projects we have studied.
- To propose cultural and social capital guidelines for designing effective development programmes.

Theoretical and methodological approach

In order to assess the cultural profile of Uganda in comparison with other countries, we measured seven cultural value orientations on which national cultures are discriminated (Schwartz, 1999, 2003). .Briefly, national cultures differ in the degree to which they emphasise:

Embeddedness maintaining the status quo, propriety, and restraint of actions or inclinations that might disrupt the solidary group or the traditional order in which people are embedded.

Intellectual autonomy the desirability of individuals pursuing their own ideas and intellectual directions independently.

Affective autonomy the desirability of individuals pursuing affectively positive experience.

Hierarchy the legitimacy of an unequal distribution of power, roles and resources.

Egalitarianism transcendence of selfish interests in favour of voluntary commitment to promoting the welfare of others.

Mastery getting ahead through active self-assertion.

Harmony fitting harmoniously into the social and natural environment.

Schwartz (1999) summarises these seven value orientations as forming three dimensions:

Embeddedness versus autonomy focuses on the nature and sources of the identity of societal members in relation to their groups. In high embeddedness cultures, people find personal meaning and significance in their identification with their groups and in the pursuit of group goals. In high autonomy cultures, in contrast, people find personal meaning and significance in cultivating their own unique intellectual and emotional capacities.

Hierarchy versus egalitarianism focuses on how to govern productive relations within society, thereby assuring responsible social behaviour that gets necessary tasks done. In high egalitarian cultures, people are socialised to internalise a commitment to the welfare of others out of a recognition of human interdependence and moral equality. In high hierarchy cultures, people's positions in hierarchical social structures are used to motivate them to meet role obligations.

Mastery versus harmony focuses on the place of humankind in the natural and social world. In high mastery cultures, the emphasis is on active control and change of the social and natural environment in order to progress. In high harmony cultures, the emphasis is on maintaining peace and harmony, co-existing with people and nature as they are rather than trying to change them.

To examine whether individual values relate to participation or non-participation in projects, and levels of success in the projects, we employed the theory of individual value systems developed by Schwartz (1992). This theory defines individual values as desirable, trans-situational goals, varying in importance, that serve as guiding principles in people's lives. It defines ten value types that are dynamically related to one another since actions taken in the pursuit of each type of values have psychological, practical, and social consequences that may conflict or may be compatible with the pursuit of other value types. The content of individual values is the type of motivational goal they express. These ten value types were arrived at by analysing the inter-correlations between the importance ratings for the total set of 57 values using the appropriate statistics (Feather, 1994).

In our study, cultural and individual values were measured with two survey instruments designed by Schwartz. The first is the Schwartz Value Survey (SVS) (Schwartz, 1992), which includes 56 or 57 single values, each followed by a brief parenthetical explanation. Respondents indicate the importance of each value as a guiding principle in their own lives, using a 9-point scale (see Chapter 4 for details of how this instrument was administered in the study). The second survey instrument called the Portraits Values Questionnaire (PVQ) was designed specifically for less educated populations. The version of this instrument we used presents brief descriptions of 29 different people. Each portrait consists of two sentences that characterise the person's goals, aspirations, and wishes, all expressive of a single value. We administered the PVQ to the participants and non-participants (control group) in the development projects in each of the regions and districts we studied (see details of this instrument and how it was administered in Chapter 4).

Social capital is another variable we used to study poverty and escaping poverty. Social capital is a characteristic of communities as well as of individuals (Putnam,

1993; Briggs, 1998). As a community characteristic, social capital refers to features of social organisation, such as trust, norms, and networks that can improve the efficiency of society by facilitating co-ordinated actions (Putnam, 1993 p.167). As an individual characteristic, social capital is an individual's capacity to access resources for growth and social support particularly in a crisis. It has also been termed social leverage (Briggs, 1998). We used nine indicators to measure social capital in a community, drawing on Putnam et al, (1993), Coleman (1988), and Uphoff (2000) in particular. For the purpose of our study, the following characteristics represent social capital in a community:

- When members share similar cognitions for which they develop supporting structures.
- When members are able to trust each other and to perform acts of reciprocity.
- When members engage in voluntary activities that serve their individual interests by increasing community resources.
- When members trust each other enough to regularly engage in wide ranging conversations.
- When members are able to form and to belong to a variety of associations.
- When members expect to be treated and are treated as equals within the community.
- When members feel optimistic enough about their community to want to invest in it.
- When members have information they are willing to share that is useful in invigorating their community.
- When members are able to link their community to the outside world.

Measuring project participation

Participation in specific development projects has a history of concrete experiences of failure to promote growth over three decades in Africa (1950s through to the 1970s) (Paul, 1990). Individuals have participated in a variety of ways ranging from sharing in benefits, implementating project objectives, evaluating outcomes, and decision-making (Cohen & Uphoff, 1980). Consider different potential levels of participation and the different objectives and modes of activity with which they are associated (Paul, 1990). The highest objective is empowerment, enabling community members to participate by giving them increased control over regulative institutions and resources. This objective is achieved when consumers and users initiate actions relevant to their own needs. The community then becomes the owner-manager of the activity. A more limited objective is capacity-building. In this case, beneficiaries take on management responsibilities such as routine decision-making, but the project is initiated from outside. A third level objective is to increase the effectiveness of a project measured in terms of goal attainment. In this case, beneficiaries are involved as much as possible in the ongoing activities on the assumption that this fosters a better match between project services and beneficiary needs. The lowest level objective is cost-sharing. This improves the efficiency of a project because involvement enhances collective understanding and agreement (Paul, 1990).

In this study we measured participation at the project level and at the household level. To measure participation at the project level, we asked respondents to indicate whether they were involved in initiation, management and implementation of the project. We also inquired whether respondents were consulted on the projects when they were being introduced in the area or whether they were just informed about the project. At the household level we determined who made decisions regarding the proceeds of the project and the purchase of inputs.

We undertook to estimate whether or not the sample that participated in the various development projects we studied changed their lives for the better as a result of participation. For this purpose, we used the increasingly important people-centred parameters that specify what constitutes a decent human existence (Sen, 1997). We chose this approach because results of two recent local studies revealed that conventional indicators of benefit were inadequate.

One study (Snyder, 2000) showed that the greatest contribution to Uganda's economy did not result from women expanding their businesses, the usual outcome measured. Rather, women contributed more by keeping their children in school and in good health through the provision of decent meals and health care. A second Ugandan study (Namatovu, 2001) compared successful and less successful village banks in an international micro-finance organisation. The official indicators of success were fulfilling obligations like paying off loans in time, holding regular bank meeting in accordance with formal regulations, and meeting statutory investments. However, the study found such success did not translate into greater business growth among participants. The indicators that did favour participants in the more successful village banks were instead found in people-centred indicators such as number of children attending school, number and type of meals households could afford, and so on.

Generally, the best indicators of change for the better were what people learned to do for themselves and their families as a result of joining the projects rather than business expansion or acquisition of material goods. The best indicators referred to capabilities acquired rather than to increased wealth. In this study, we looked for evidence of whether project participants had learned to live more effectively rather than evidence of commodity acquisition. We looked for interpersonal and intrapersonal learning and for indicators of qualitative development change that would distinguish between those who had gained as a result of participation and those who had not (see also Sen, 1997).

The study design had two major phases. We tested the validity of the theory of values in the Ugandan context in the first phase. To do this we used teacher (n = 478) and student (n = 478) samples to answer the SVS. In the second phase we used the PVQ to assess cultural and individual values of project participants (n = 293) and a control group of non-project members (n = 105). We also interviewed project and non-project participants on a number of issues concerning why they do or do not participate and whether participants were involved in the initiation, implementation or management of the project. We asked what features of the projects were attractive or unattractive. We inquired about decision-making at the household level with reference to project proceeds and so on. Considerable time was also spent in examining secondary data on poverty and gender in Uganda in general and in the selected districts in particular.

The samples were obtained from seven districts varying in socio-economic development, from three regions of Uganda. From the Western region we selected Bushenyi and Kabale. From the Northern region we used Arua and Nebbi. In the Central region we used Mpigi, Mukono, and Masaka. Bushenyi, from the West, Arua, in the North and Mpigi in the Central region represented the higher social economic status in their respective regions.

How the book is organised

We deal with the problem of poverty and escaping poverty in the seven following chapters. Chapter 2 describes the Ugandan experience of poverty, with particular attention to gender differences in poverty and to the ways individual poor people themselves, experience and perceive poverty. We introduce the construct of the social psychological individual in order to emphasise the need to understand how the poor interact continuously with others, deliberately forming and drawing upon social networks to ensure their own survival. Among the other deliberate actions of the poor that must be understood are the short-term tactical decisions they make and the longer-term strategies they employ to preserve their limited resources or improve their situation. In this respect we introduce the concept of poverty carriers, the acts that perpetuate or produce poverty, acts that must change if individuals are to escape poverty. Such acts as selling one's piece of land, one's own labour, or one's children's labour are strategic acts that firmly place individuals and households on the road to poverty. We have suggested that, in order to develop successful methods for alleviating poverty, it is necessary to uncover the specific acts in the daily lives of the poor that lead to the outcomes typically viewed as indicators of poverty (i.e. level of income, housing conditions, calorie consumption). We recommended that researchers and policy-makers closely observe and listen to these individuals who are found in the streets trying to hawk their wares, selling cooked food, sitting in crowded markets, and walking to their place of work. If these poverty-carrying acts are identified, academics and practitioners can more easily design policies and studies to target the offending acts directly.

In Chapter 3, we discuss culture as a necessary but not sufficient condition for development. We distinguish between weak and strong cultures (Gyekye, 1997). We examine culture as the context in which growth and development take place and discuss African culture and modernity, starting from the African philosophical anthropology framework. We present a model of cultural values to illustrate the meaning and importance of culture as a source of motivation expressed in values at both the community and individual levels. We finally introduce the concept of the cultural interface to emphasise a point that in Africa the operative culture is mainly defined by the recent intensive cultural contact between colonising and host cultures. We provide examples of negative and positive cultural interfaces, including social capital, as behavioural manifestations of underlying cultural values. Cultural interfaces are the coming together of institutions or cultural elements. Their critical components or elements are the patterned beliefs, values and practices that individuals are predisposed to take for granted, accept and defend or to reject and ignore.

In Chapter 4 we present empirical findings using a recent theory of values with data from over 6000 respondents in as many as 65 countries from all inhabited continents.

We also use the model of cultural value dimensions to provide a detailed comparison of cultural values in Uganda to other countries and to examine cultural values in the Ugandan districts and regions we studied, each with its particular ethnic composition. Thirdly, we consider individual rather than cultural values and examine the relation of individual differences in values to participation in development projects and to economic performance and success.

In Chapter 5 we examine how people act within the context of their social networks, how they learn from these networks and alter them. The chapter first examines the nature of social networks and networking. It then shows how development depends on networking. Finally, it presents and discusses data on how Ugandan peasants who were attempting to escape poverty established and utilised networks and networking.

One of the central characteristics of networks and networking is people-generated participation. In Chapter 6 we discuss our data in the light of this kind of participation and relate it to the performance measures we adopted for use in the projects about which we report. The chapter is divided into two sections. The first section briefly discusses participation by distinguishing between system maintaining and system transforming participation. The second section draws upon the data collected in the study to demonstrate the relevance of participation in selected project outcomes to escaping poverty.

In Chapter 7 we address social capital as a vehicle for moving out of poverty and introduce the concept of value-based social capital, again drawing on Schwartz's value theory and measures. In the process, we provide a limited review of the ever-growing literature of social capital (Woolcock & Narayan, 2000). In the second part of the chapter, we examine data from our samples relating social capital to their attempts at moving out of poverty. In keeping with the general analysis model we have adopted in this work, we present a limited quantitative set of data to serve two purposes. First we try to quantify our understanding of social capital within the Ugandan context. We then link our concept of value-based social capital to some of the measures of performance discussed in Chapter 6. Lastly we concentrate on qualitative analysis and presentation in order to examine the process of either becoming poor or escaping poverty and to illustrate the relevance of social capital in this process.

Chapter 8 puts together in a generalised form what we set out to examine and to understand. This is the person trying to move out of poverty, the individual-in-development, or the social psychological individual. We propose that the onset of poverty is traceable to poverty carriers, actions performed by or done to an individual /community that adversely affect the optimal utilisation of productive resources in the short, medium, or long term. The social psychology of development focuses on those poverty-carrying actions done by the individual but also examines those done to the individual by an outside agent. The foundation of what an individual can do is determined or prescribed by cultural learning. Cultural learning refers to what an individual can do in co-operation with others in his or her community and not necessarily what he or she can do alone (Vygotsky, 1978). We introduce the concept of *zones of proximal development* (Vygotsky, 1978). The zone of proximal development is the distance between the level of development people actually attain based on independent problem solving and the level they could potentially attain through problem solving under adult guidance or in collaboration with more capable peers (Vygotsky, p. 86, 1978). This is the context in which cultural learning or learning how to develop takes place. Its effectiveness depends on the dominant cultural interface that is attendant in the zone. Some of the interfaces will conflict when parties that compose the zone of proximal development bring with them institutions that are opposed to them. Others will be harmonious when the institutions parties bring to the zone are harmonious. Cultural values are the key determinants of cultural interfaces between African societies and their donor nations and a systematic study of the cultures of the two parties is essential as long as Africa still relies on donor nations and /or Euro-American markets for selling and buying produce and other resources. One cultural interface we identified that is harmonious is what is referred to as social capital. A study of the individual-in-development should clarify the social capital that exists in the community of interest. There are also three generically negative cultural interfaces that should be clarified at the onset of any development programme. These are: gender role, economy of affection, and attribution of causation. Finally the process of escaping poverty is essentially one of interaction rather than action. Therefore a study of poverty and the subsequent policy to alleviate poverty, should focus on the networks that prevent people from taking actions that can initiate and maintain well-being. The book ends with a look at how networks, zones of proximal development, and cultural interface all play a part in successful strategies for poverty alleviation.

---

1. A small kerosene candle locally made and notorious for polluting a house with soot in excess of the light it produces.
2. In a perspective on poverty we do not elaborate, Harrison (1982) proposed that it be considered in terms of four sources and manifestations, geographical, social, economic and political.
3. These are value expressive advantages. Their competitive advantage holds only to the extent that the underlying values are competitive with the values of the beneficiaries/stakeholders especially in the case of development as opposed to relief oriented NGOs.

2
The Poor in Africa with
Special Reference to Uganda

The aspect of poverty that has come to dominate poverty and development debates is the low income of the poor. Because economists have been most prominent in the study of development and poverty, non-economic outcomes are less well understood or even recognised (Afonja &Aina, 1995). Consequently, we must begin our discussion of poverty in Uganda with its economic manifestations. This chapter is divided into two sections. Section One considers income-oriented manifestations of poverty. Section Two discusses the more qualitative manifestations of being poor in Uganda.

Ugandan poverty profile: A view from national statistical sources[1]

Ugandans rarely tell interviewers what they earn, but they do report what they spend.[2] Accordingly, to measure the economic level of the poor, we asked about household and per capita monthly expenditures. Table 2.1 presents the results. It shows that Mpigi district is the richest of the seven districts we studied and Nebbi is the poorest. The districts with the highest household expenditures (Masaka, Mpigi, and Mukono) are all in the Central region, followed by the Western districts (Bushenyi and Kabale). The two Northern districts are the poorest.

The table also reveals that female-headed households spend less than male-headed households in every one of the districts. On average, male-headed households spend 91,245 shillings per month, whereas female-headed household spend 72,723 shillings, a difference of 25%. The gender difference in favour of male-headed households in the poorest district (Nebbi) is 40%. The columns labelled Z-score provide another view of differences between districts and genders. These scores are standardised around the average of all districts. A positive score means that spending in a district is above the average, a negative score means that spending is below the average. The larger the positive or negative score the more or less spending is above or below the average respectively. The Z-scores show that spending is above the average in all Central region districts and below the average in all other districts.

Another good indicator of poverty is the proportion of money a household or an individual spends on food relative to other items. The higher the proportion devoted to food and drink, the greater the poverty. Table 2.2 shows relative poverty among the seven districts using this indicator.

As expected, the relatively poorer districts and female-headed households spend proportionally more on food items than the relatively more well-to-do districts and male-headed households. Thus, in Mpigi, male-headed and female-headed households spent 25% and 30% on food, respectively, as compared to Nebbi, where over 80% of spending was devoted to food regardless of the gender of the household head. The

16

Table 2.1: Selected district average monthly expenditure per household and per capita 1997*

District	Male-headed households				Female-headed households				Total	
	Household	Z-score	Per capita	Z-score	Household	Z-score	Per capita	Z-score	Household	Per capita
Bushenyi	83,620	-0.34	23,844	-0.51	71,475	-.088	6,617	-0.34	80,527	15,011
Kabale	80,854	-0.46	23,573	-0.55	60,515	-0.87	5,497	-0.69	76,097	14,627
Arua	74,312	-0.76	22,099	-0.78	67,403	-0.38	4,741	-0.92	72,948	13,247
Nebbi	73,956	-0.77	22,436	-0.72	52,916	-1.40	4,168	-1.10	69,659	13,355
Mukono	94,075	0.12	29,852	0.41	82,187	0.67	10,114	0.73	90,815	20,113
Masaka	93,903[1]	0.11	27,979	0.12	80,357	0.54	10,877	0.97	89,541	19,237
Mpigi	138,064	2.00	40,518	2.00	94,211	1.50	12,085	1.40	125,108	26,596
Average	91,245		27,186		72,723		7,728		86,385	17,455

* In Uganda shillings at an exchange rate of Shs 1,750- to the US dollar

Table 2.2: Percentage of total household expenditures devoted to food and drink by district and sex of household head in 1997

Region	District	Male-headed household	Female-headed household
Western	Bushenyi	64%	64%
	Kabale	63%	61%
Northern	Arua	64%	73%
	Nebbi	84%	92%
Central	Mukono	48%	62%
	Masaka	54%	62%
	Mpigi	25%	30%

differences in spending on food are much more pronounced among districts than between male-headed and female-headed households within districts. Indeed, in Kabale, male-headed households spend more on food than female-headed households.

We also examined the distribution of income in the three regions. Gini coefficients of 0.42 in the Central region, 0.51 in the Western region and 0.54 in the Northern region (Okwi & Kaija, 2000) indicate that the distribution of wealth in the Central region is relatively more equitable than in the other two regions.

Another important poverty carrier is illiteracy, the inability to read and write. Levels of illiteracy are consistent with the indicators of poverty discussed above. Table 2.3 reveals that more female heads of households are illiterate than males in every district. The gender differences in illiteracy average 36%, but they vary greatly across districts, from only 18% in Mpigi to 56% in Arua and Nebbi. Thus, it is the poorer districts that also show the largest gender differences. Illiteracy levels vary much less across districts for male-headed than for female-headed households.

Another interesting poverty carrier on which statistics are available is the main income-generating activity engaged in by heads of households. Crop farming, the most common activity, is usually a subsistence level activity that leaves people trapped in poverty. As shown in Table 2.4, crop farming is least common in the relatively more economically advantaged district, Mpigi, for both male- and female-headed households (42% and 56% respectively). Crop farming is much more prevalent as the main income generating

Table 2.3: Proportion of household heads who are illiterate by district and by sex

Region	District	Male-headed household	Female-headed household
Western	Bushenyi	34%	65%
	Kabale	25%	70%
Northern	Arua	21%	77%
	Nebbi	30%	86%
Central	Mukono	26%	50%
	Masaka	25%	45%
	Mpigi	14%	32%

Table 2.4: Percentage of household heads engaging in main income-generating activity 1997

Region	District	Household head sex	% of type of income-generating activity		
			Crop farming	Other	No activity
Western	Bushenyi	Male	69	34	7
		Female	82	14	4
	Kabale	Male	62	31	7
		Female	78	8	14
Northern	Arua	Male	84	12	4
		Female	78	8	14
	Nebbi	Male	77	21	2
		Female	71	14	15
Central	Mukono	Male	52	43	5
		Female	60	23	17
	Masaka	Male	60	36	4
		Female	69	28	13
	Mpigi	Male	42	53	5
		Female	56	37	7

activity in relatively poorer districts like Arua and Nebbi. In all the other districts surveyed, female household heads are more likely to engage in crop farming than male household heads, reinforcing the picture that Arua and Nebbi are more disadvantaged. Engaging in other income-generating activities such as trading is more likely to provide resources to enable individuals to move out of poverty. Such activities are more common in the Mpigi district and among male household heads, a further sign of their relatively advantaged state.

Ugandan poverty profile: A view from qualitative sources

The statistical picture presented above defines the scope of poverty. As background for designing ways to overcome the problems of poverty, we now examine processes through which individuals and communities become poor and the critical activities that prevent their escape. We present a theoretical analysis of these processes in subsequent chapters. Here we summarise what is known of these processes from published literature on Uganda and review the findings of studies of qualitative characteristics of poverty.

Table 2.5 below sums up the work done by an NGO that focuses on poverty alleviation in the same seven districts we studied. The study also included Kampala, in order to incorporate the urban area. The objectives of the survey included establishing the basic characteristics of poverty in communities, examining some elements of the evolution of poverty there, collecting local perceptions of poverty, and learning about the coping strategies of the poor. The study employed participatory methods such as social and resource mapping, transect walks, seasonal calendars, wealth ranking and problem preference ranking.

Table 2.5 presents ideas from two of the poverty perspectives discussed in Chapter One. Column 1 lists poverty-carrying activities, in keeping with the action perspective on poverty. Column 2 describes the conditions from which the poor suffer, in keeping with the state of being (or personal attributes) perspective. Column 3 outlines two strategies that individuals employed to move out of poverty. Column 4 summarises the recommendations made by the NGO that conducted the study.

As shown in column 1, there were two main categories of poverty carriers in this study. The first is the use of existing resources by the poor in ways that eventually reduce their productivity. The examples we identified include putting children to labour and intensifying women's workload by selling food crops for cash. For example, putting children to labour limits their opportunities to reach their full physical and intellectual potential, thereby reducing their competitiveness as adults. In Africa, where there is no welfare state, competitive children are a crucial asset. Parents depend on their grown children to help them in difficult times (e.g. famines), to contribute to major family projects (e.g. building a house), and to look after them when they are old. Parents who fail to send their children to school so that they can reach their full potential, condemn both themselves and their children to poverty in the long run and in general.

The second main category of actions that promote poverty is the actual disposal of productive assets. This includes selling one's labour for a non-competitive fee, lending or selling portions of land, and selling food crops. In a predominantly agricultural society, all these actions push those who perform them further into the grip of poverty and increase their desperation. By selling the land and labour they control, the poor use up the means of production that are essential to alleviate individual and household poverty. Such actions are the true carriers of poverty and, as we will see later, such poverty-carrying actions are often related to community, district, or national level poverty-carrying events. A serious assault on poverty in Africa will require identifying poverty-carrying actions and dealing with them systematically. The case below provides a telling example of how the poor become poorer by underselling the few means of production they control.

Column 2 of Table 2.5 lists various factors that indicate an individual state of poverty.

Case study 2.1: Selling labour

Akiiki is a mother of three whose husband was retrenched during the 1993 Uganda Public Service retrenching exercise. Frustrated, the man took to drink. Akiiki then migrated with her nine-month old baby to Kampala, where she found employment as a housemaid. Her monthly pay was approximately five dollars, but she needed a minimum of ten dollars. To cope, she took a two-month advance and lived permanently in debt to her employer. She was not able to send money back home, nor was she able to travel to see her other two children. She felt trapped.

Source: Community Development Resource Network, 1996. A Study of Poverty in Selected Districts of Uganda. Kampala.

Table 2.5: Poverty carriers and poverty indicators: A seven district poverty study

(1) Poverty carrying activities	(2) Poverty indicators	(3) Strategies of growth	(4) Recommendations
Poverty promoting use of existing resources. Putting children to labour. Intensifying women's workload by selling food crops for cash. Disposing of productive assets. Selling one's labour. Lending portions of one's land. Selling land.	Lack of social support. Social exclusion. Nuclearisation of families. Lack of relatives. Being on poor terms with neighbours. Loss of traditional values. Not being at peace with oneself. Poor housing conditions. Lack of food security. Having not more than one meal a day. Lack of cash to buy clothing. Reduced access to health and education. Inability to cope with disease. Inability to engage in land-based activities.	Finding external sources of incomes through formal employment. Joining the second-hand clothing trade.	Formulate policy with the active participation of the poor. Keep the poor informed of strategic developments such as debt, military spending, etc. Make the poverty debate as central as the AIDS and gender debates. Balance macro and micro policies when dealing with poverty. Target the gender dimension in poverty programmes. Focus on infrastructure. Mainstream small-holder producers into agriculture and other investment policies.

Source: Community Development Resource Network (1996). A Study of Poverty in Selected Districts of Uganda

To understand what is happening to the poor it is often necessary to deconstruct these indicators. This enables us to discover what actions by the poor have contributed to the state they are in. Consider the indicator of social isolation. The question is how did poor people come to be socially isolated? How did they come to lose the social networks from which they should draw support in times of need? Why are they separated from their extended family and close friends? If we are to alleviate the poverty that ensues from social isolation, we need to answer these questions. One critical action is migration in search of new opportunities. Although this action is intended to lead to an escape from poverty, migrants often lack leverage and resources such as social support to help them succeed in their new environment.[3]

We deconstruct Akiiki's social isolation as an example. Her isolation began when her husband failed to deal effectively with his retrenchment. Needing a helping hand from others, she apparently failed to find sufficient social support in her own community. What Akiiki lacked was social capital. Social capital is the capacity of individuals to draw upon others in times of need and the capacity of communities to offer help. When the only resources Akiiki had left were her unskilled labour, she moved to a new community where she could sell her labour. This decision, taken due to a lack of social capital, drew Akiiki deeper into poverty. It brought conditions associated with poverty upon her. She could no longer live up to the traditional value of caring for the young children she had left at home because she had no money to send them or to travel to visit them. As a result, she probably found it difficult to live at peace with herself.

Akiiki's situation is replayed time and again in different scenarios among rural and urban women in Uganda and elsewhere. Such cases have led to a number of policy-oriented studies focusing on the gender dimension of poverty (Afonja & Aina, 1995; Narayan, 1997). Later we explore this literature to identify the actions and events that make women consistently poorer than men.

Returning to Table 2.5 column 3 presents strategies the poor in this study employed in their attempt to escape poverty. Those who were able, sought formal employment. Some others, who could not find formal employment, joined the second-hand clothing trade, the most lucrative and non-perishable trade for petty traders. This second option is interesting because it requires a specific set of actions: using what little formal education one may have, finding and drawing upon contacts, and learning from them the details of the trade. Though the study did not clarify how formal education was useful, it did reveal that contacts were used to access some credit, to learn how to buy bales of second-hand clothes, and to find space in a trading centre from which to operate. A recent study which interviewed petty traders in Kampala (Snyder, 2000) reported that many poor people begin their trading with perishables, such as serving cooked food on the roadside. Those who accumulate or can access enough capital then move on to non-perishable foodstuffs and eventually to second-hand clothing. Thus, the choice of second-hand clothing is an apt, goal-directed, strategy.

The recommendations in column 4 of Table 2.5 build on what the researchers learned from listening to the poor themselves. The first policy recommendation is central to poverty alleviation in Africa: the poor have much to contribute to formulating policy on poverty. The example of moving into the second-hand clothing trade illustrates how strategies that come from the poor themselves are most appropriate. Poor people were able to put their minimal education and contacts to work acquiring relevant knowledge and skills that fit their own capabilities. They provided simple but workable ideas that demonstrated a high degree of motivation to achieve. They were able to articulate their needs, to recognise the risks involved in moving up the trading ladder, and to accept these risks because they appeared manageable in their own day-to-day context. Failure to draw on the ideas of poor people when formulating poverty alleviation policies has probably contributed greatly to the continued poverty in Africa.

Another recommendation that merits comment is the importance of finding a balance between macro- and micro-policies when dealing with poverty. Experiments with over half-a-dozen macro-policies centred on growth have been carried out in Uganda and the rest of Africa (Sandbrook, 1982; Bisi & Aina, 1995). What we have not had in sufficient numbers are trials of micro-policies. To plan these, policy-makers must first acquire an intimate understanding of the daily activities of those whom they are targeting and of their surrounding environment. Moreover, the focus of such policies must move from outcomes (e.g., income levels) down to the goal-directed actions of the poor (e.g., how they generate income). The poor themselves have much to tell policy-makers about their daily actions and struggle. The chapters in this book on social capital, networking, and participation all focus on these actions.

We next draw on the most recent study of poverty in Uganda (MFPED, 2000) to discover how the poor themselves describe who is poor, what are their characteristics, and what makes them so (Table 2.6 a, b). We also analyse the implications of these perceptions for policy solutions. Some perceptions focus on material conditions, others on the actions that the individual, household, or community do or do not perform. Still other perceptions focus on the enduring social attributes of the individual, household, or community, the event-states of poverty.

The first seven perceptions in Table 2.6 (a) (p.24) indicate relatively enduring conditions that describe a poor individual. These are terminal or permanent conditions that are difficult to change, pointing to a hopeless situation. The policies relevant in such cases are generic or blueprint policies that have been tried elsewhere to provide relief.

Reading the table from left to right, we take any description we are interested in and find where a symbol Y is placed. This indicates our interpretation of this perception in terms of what it means and what policy implication it has. Thus, perceptions 8-15 reflect the same kind of hopelessness and helplessness as identified in the case of Akiiki, this time applied to poor households and communities. The households are described as destitute and starving, the community as lacking the critical resources to survive. These perceptions identify end-states or outcomes. They do not identify the actions that have brought the households and communities to their present state of poverty. Those who try to help the poor based on such perceptions are likely to propose generic or blueprint strategies such as relief. Blueprint strategies are based on a good understanding of poverty indicators such as poverty lines but a poor appreciation of poverty carriers. As noted above, they are unlikely to bring sustainable improvements. Moreover, they run the risk of making the poor dependent. Much can be gained if studies pay less attention to outcomes and end-result conditions and instead build a theory of poverty based on what people do and do not do.

Perceptions 16 to 33 (Table 2.6 (b), p.26) tell us, in varying degrees, what it is that the poor people in the UPPAP sample do. Some perceptions give sufficient background

Table 2.6 (a) End-state perceptions of poverty

Selected local perceptions of poverty	Outcome conditions that suggest generic or blueprint policies	Event state	Most likely poverty alleviation strategy
1. Aged and helpless due to loss of all one's children	Y	Y	Relief
2. Aged and weak because of helplessness	Y	Y	Relief
3. Aged with orphans wh they cannot materially support	Y	Y	Relief
4. Being a widow or a widower without property	Y	Y	Relief
6. Being without a father or mother			
7. Broken marriages due to family quarrels, arising from food shortages and other basic needs	Y / Y	Y / Y	Relief / Relief
8. Low standard at the prevailing sub-county secondary school	Y	Y	Relief
9. Low standard of education			
10. Low tax base	Y	Y	Relief
11. Malaria on the increase	Y	Y	Relief
12. No funds at sub-county	Y	Y	Relief
13. No rural credit	Y	Y	Relief
14. Not having enough food for the family	Y	Y	Relief
15. The community is landless, many people lack land on which to grow food	Y / Y / Y	Y / Y / Y	Relief / Relief / Relief

to reveal initial poverty-carrying actions. For example, number 17 tells us that households may be poor because there are many wives who compete for the few available resources. We can infer some of the discrete actions that may cause poverty in such households; actions the household members have the power to change. First is the act of marrying many wives, followed by acting competitively rather than sharing co-operatively. Though perception 17 did not specify the kinds of resources for which the wives compete, other research suggests that the resources are not necessarily material, at least initially (Matovu, 1995).

In a study of the effectiveness of the heifer project[4] for Ugandan women farmers, Matovu (1995) found that competition for status in polygamous families led to poverty in some cases or prevented households from escaping poverty. Matovu evaluated the success of the project in terms of what it contributed to emancipating the woman farmer socially and economically. In both monogamous and polygamous families, she found that the relationship between husband and wife strongly affected whether the project succeeded or failed. Where women had poor social relations, especially with their husbands, prior to the project, the project failed to achieve its major objective of emancipation. Indeed, providing women with a heifer exacerbated the already deteriorating situation. One of many illustrative cases is reproduced on page 28 (Matovu, 1995, pp.105-106). This case demonstrates that the co-wives competed for status both before and after the farmer received the project animal.

Returning to perception 17 of Table 2.6 (b), note that it fits all aspects of the poverty descriptions derived from the common perspectives on poverty introduced in Chapter One. The perception suggests discrete actions (competing for limited resources) that contribute to poverty, and it describes a relatively enduring condition (the presence of many wives), the state of being. In addition, the mention of a few resources that the wives compete for might indicate a material definition of poverty. We therefore score the perception on both descriptions of event meaning and on the two potential policy recommendations, namely empowerment as well as capacity building. Case study 2.2 illustrates how mistaken generic solutions to poverty that focus only on increasing material and informational resources can be. Poverty in this household is due to a shortage of social resources rather than any other types of resources.

Viewing the emergence or maintenance of poverty as resulting from a series of actions and their outcomes can serve to integrate a number of different perceptions. In Table 2.6 (a), we order several perceptions in a matrix that traces the event-state of not having enough food for the family (perception 14) to various discrete action-events. For example, the state of not having enough food for the family (14) can be traced through various discrete actions or events. The most distant but fundamental cause may be being a bad farmer (19) (Table 2.6 (b), p.26). This is related to using inappropriate farm technology (18), which, in turn, reflects the use of child labour (16). Together these mean that there is a lack of inputs (22) and therefore low agricultural production: not enough food is grown to feed the family (14). The reader may note that it is possible to reconstruct the events in Tables 2.6 (a) and (b) in ways different from our reconstructions. What is important is to arrange the events in a reasonable chronological order that can ultimately reveal potential points of intervention in this farmer's life.

Table 2.6 (b) Action-based perceptions of poverty

Selected local perceptions of poverty	Event-actions that contribute to poverty and can be changed	Event-action	Event-state	Most likely poverty alleviation strategy
16. Using child labour to provide for the family's subsistence	Y	Y		Capacity-building and empowerment
17. A household with many wives, since they compete for the few resources	Y	Y	Y	Capacity-building and empowerment
18. Absence of approprite farm technology	Y	Y	Y	Capacity-building and empowerment
19. Being a bad farmer	Y	Y		Capacity-building and empowerment
20. Lack of ownership of a forest from which to get firewood and timber for sale.	Y	Y	Y	Capacity-building and empowerment
21. Lacks employment that provides enough income which could be invested.	Y	Y	Y	Capacity-building and empowerment
22. Low agricultural production because of lack of inputs for agriculture.	Y	Y	Y	Capacity-building and empowerment
23. Soil infertility, due to over-use, soil erosion and landslides.	Y	Y	Y	Capacity-building and empowerment
24. Too many people to look after due to lack of family planning.	Y	Y	Y	Capacity-building and empowerment
25. Traditional ceremonies finishing resources in granaries and home.	Y	Y	Y	Capacity-building and empowerment
26. Women avoid growing crops for sale because of lack of ownership of land.	Y	Y	Y	Capacity-building and empowerment
27. Youth migrating to town to look for casual labour, leading to labour deficits in the community	Y	Y	Y	Capacity-building
28. Being ignorant	Y		Y	Capacity-building
29. Being uneducated.				
30. Little land, limiting the production capability of households.	Y	Y	Y	Capacity-building
31. Not educating children.	Y	Y		Capacity-building
32. Not having a banana plantation.	Y	Y		Capacity-building
33. Not having commercial enterprises	Y	Y		Capacity-building

All the perceptions of poverty in this example point either explicitly or implicitly to behaviours that can be changed. This has clear implications for designing practical policies to deal with the specific poverty scenarios. It is much more difficult to design practical policies based only on knowledge of outcomes. That requires trying to guess the causes of the outcomes and the behaviours that require change. Perceptions of the poor that do not at least imply the actions that keep the poor in poverty are of limited use to those who want to alleviate poverty in Africa. However, such perceptions are not uncommon. Of 382 perceptions mentioned in the UPPAP study, 50 simply described outcomes (e.g.1-15 in Table 2.6 (a)). However, many other perceptions of poverty that the poor themselves supplied did describe relevant actions. These may be used to design better policies and solutions than many of those proposed in the 40 years since African independence. Policies based on what the poor do are more likely to address tangible poverty carriers and the processes that perpetuate poverty.

The condition of the poor farmer exemplifies what those interested in fighting poverty need to do. They need to shift their attention from end results (poverty in general), like not having enough food for the family, to those activities that can jointly explain why or how that end-result came about. Only when these activities and processes are understood is it time to proceed to search for solutions and propose policies. In the farmer's case, the appropriate policies would be to build his capacity and to empower him to change his poverty-carrying behaviours. As noted earlier, without knowledge of the activities that carry poverty, well-meaning policy-makers often propose generic or blueprint policies.

In concluding this section, we reiterate the importance of spending time with the poor, trying to understand from direct interaction with them the destructive and constructive actions they perform and the social contexts in which they act. Descriptions that merely spell out the condition of the poor, like 1 to 15 in Table 2.6 (a), are no more useful than quantitative statistical descriptions of the poor. Like these, qualitative

Figure 2.1: Some causes and consequences of being a poor farmer

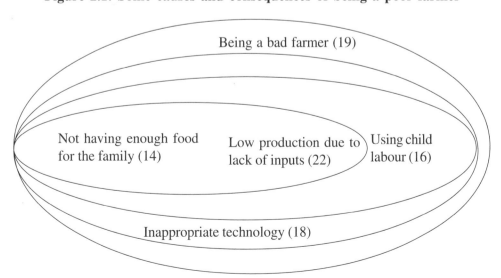

descriptions of end results provide no direct indication of underlying processes. Instead, they lead to generic policies that are not tailored to specific situations, policies that have failed to relieve increasing poverty in Africa. The alternative is to try to deconstruct the summary statistics or qualitative descriptions of end-states to figure out what actions lie behind them. We contend that a better solution is to focus initially on activities and processes, as attempted in the UPPAP (MFED, 2000). However, the UPPAP provided only basic data. The real work of uncovering the causal relations among process events and outcome conditions is still to be done. With the advance in computer assisted qualitative data analysis the laborious work of piecing together an understanding of poverty at the level of everyday experience can, however, be substantially reduced.

Gender and poverty in Uganda

The most studied group difference in poverty in Uganda is that between women and men. Consistent with the data we cited, there is consensus that more Ugandan women than men live below the poverty line, although differences in education rather than gender may account for this differential. The presumed greater poverty of women has led to a concerted effort to target women, especially in the rural areas. One such effort

Case study 2.2: Competing for status in a polygamous family

B is a 38-year-old woman farmer who is one of the two wives of a 45-year-old man. Both wives live under one roof. B is the second and younger wife. She was also the favourite prior to receiving the heifer. Before the project began, the two wives had not co-operated and had personal quarrels because the husband had favoured B.

B received a Friesian cow with the assistance of her husband who contributed capital to start the project. He also helped in milking and marketing the milk produced. At this early stage, B handled all the income without interference from the husband. Her income increased her status in the home, widened the gap between her and the co-wife, and increased the hostility between them. This led to physical violence between the co-wives and, subsequently, between B and her husband. When the two wives had a physical fight over status in the home, the husband punished B physically because he blamed her for provoking the fight. He then humiliated B by removing the project animal from her care and taking control of it himself. He dismissed the labourer that B had hired and demanded that B perform all the project tasks.

At the time of the study, B looked overworked and miserable because she was required to perform all the household and project tasks. She said that the project had increased the problems in the household. "At the beginning I was happy and worked hard to earn this money. Now my husband takes all the money. He did this because he believed that with that money I had become stubborn and independent. I am no longer interested in the project that is why I don't even keep records of how much milk we get. I cannot even dress properly to go to project meetings because I don't have clothes to wear. My mother is very sick, but I cannot even travel to visit her because I don't have money for transport, and when I asked my husband to give it to me, he refused.

was undertaken in Bundibugyo, a district in Western Uganda on the eastern borders of the Democratic Republic of Congo. This isolated community is approximately three hours by air from the capital of the Democratic Republic of the Congo. It is inaccessible from Kampala city, particularly during the rainy season. This puts it beyond social services from both Uganda and the Democratic Republic of Congo. In fact, the situation on the Democratic Republic of Congo border has been such that Congolese cross the border to Uganda for medical and other services. This geographical isolation has kept the communities in Bundibugyo in greater poverty than the rest of Uganda. Figure 2.2 displays the conditions that prevailed before the project, what the project tried to do, and some outcomes.

Figure 2.2 lists several ways in which women were underprivileged. For example, they were exchanged for domestic animals, they were considered merely as a source of domestic labour, they suffered from greater illiteracy than men, and they were not

**Figure 2.2: Poverty and gender inequality in Bundibugyo:
Bundibugyo Action Aid Project (BAP)**

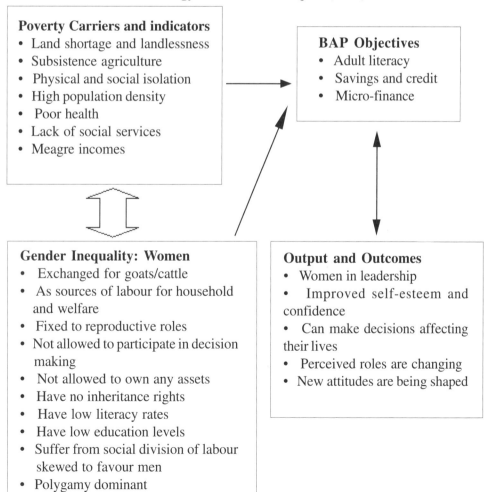

Poverty Carriers and indicators
- Land shortage and landlessness
- Subsistence agriculture
- Physical and social isolation
- High population density
- Poor health
- Lack of social services
- Meagre incomes

BAP Objectives
- Adult literacy
- Savings and credit
- Micro-finance

Gender Inequality: Women
- Exchanged for goats/cattle
- As sources of labour for household and welfare
- Fixed to reproductive roles
- Not allowed to participate in decision making
- Not allowed to own any assets
- Have no inheritance rights
- Have low literacy rates
- Have low education levels
- Suffer from social division of labour skewed to favour men
- Polygamy dominant

Output and Outcomes
- Women in leadership
- Improved self-esteem and confidence
- Can make decisions affecting their lives
- Perceived roles are changing
- New attitudes are being shaped

Case study 2.3: Statements by participants about the success of the programme

1. Through REFLECT I now know how to write my name! I can go to the bank. We women are no longer marginalised. (capability , functioning and leverage)

2. I am in class to learn how to read and write. I want to go to Kampala and marry an educated wife. (disappearing bonding capital)

Table 2.7:Gender focused poverty alleviation: Bundibugyo Actionaid Project (BAP)

(1) Objectives of BAP	(2) Output, outcomes, and impact	(3) General observation	(4) Competencies and capabilities
Facilitate the acquisition of functional literacy for 25,000 illiterates. Establish a post literacy programme for 19,500 neoliterates. Facilitate the formation of savings and credit groups for the neoliterates. Support prioritised parish initiatives. Train local leaders in project planning, management, monitoring and evaluation. Establish and manage a community-based monitoring and evaluation system, Increase accessibility to social services such as feeder roads, community-based health care and teacher education. Increase women's participation in decison-making and control over resources.	Literacy achieved, leading to self-confidence and networking. The voluntary literacy classess succeeded because access to credit was tagged on to completing the learning. New saving and credit schemes set up as a result of the presence of BAP's scheme. Community leverage such as better schools, roads and health facilities did not translate into house-hold poverty eradica-tion.	A clear gender focus top-down approach. Sustainability in question as locals make reference to BAP structures. Focus on both bridging individual and institutional leverage.	**Individual level** Literacy improved. Saving and credit introduced. Confidence built among particpants. **Household level** Women making decisions that are binding. **Community level** Creating institu-tional leverage through better schools, roads and health facilities.

allowed to make decisions about their own households. Though the carriers and indicators of poverty in Bundibugyo are similar to those in the rest of Uganda, the community's isolation makes it especially vulnerable. This has attracted donor and government support that has sought to deal with the problem by empowering individuals, households, and the community. Table 2.7 summarises such activity.

The programme had a comprehensive range of objectives as shown in column 1. It targeted women at the individual, household, and community levels. Column 2 shows that the programme succeeded in providing at least short-term leverage to all three targets. This was achieved through the use of REFLECT (Regenerated Freirean Literacy through Empowering Community Techniques) that:

- Broke the isolation of the communities by giving participants skills and knowledge derived from adult literacy.
- Increased the capacity of communities in decision-making processes so as to influence their economic, social, and political environment.
- Raised the status and confidence of marginalised groups.
- Developed community members' self-esteem.

Two statements by programme participants (Case study 2.3) exemplify the successes of the programme (Bundibugyo Actionaid Project (BAP) 1997. Midterm Review). The first reflects improved capacity to live effectively in society, a gain in capabilities and function (Sen, 1997). The second reflects a change in loyalties leading to the goal of applying one's skills outside the community. We refer to this as 'disappearing bonding capital,' a concept discussed in later chapters.

The marginalisation of women, which tends to keep them, as a group, below the poverty line, was analysed in a project dealing with micro finance and micro-enterprises (Johnson, 1996). The project identified four common reasons why women more than men tend to live below the poverty line. Table 2.8 (p.33) summarises the study.

We see again that the problems that keep women below the poverty line cover many domains of activity and are manifested at the individual, household and community/national levels. In the table, we group the manifestations of marginalisation under cultural influences. For instance, the cultural preference for educating male rather than female children ensures that more women than men are illiterate. The persistent household and community cultural practice of valuing women's decisions less than men's probably reflects low female education and the hierarchical, patriarchal system practised in Uganda.

A recent study by Snyder (2000) supports the view that emancipating women in Uganda involves changes in the patriarchy system, which places men at the top of the hierarchy. Snyder writes that by bringing men but not women into the market economy and salaried employment, the colonial era entrenched men's hold over women. By controlling the cash in a cash economy, men took away whatever power women had held in pre-colonial society. At this period in Ugandan history women became legally minors. However, the market economy that established men's control also later created opportunities for women to regain some of the status they had lost with the coming of colonialism. The oil crisis in the early seventies led to a substantial drop in real incomes at the household level. Consequently, wherever possible, women sought formal or informal employment to supplement household income. Women's employment reduced men's control over them. Table 2.9 summarises how a series of political and economic events in the world, and especially in Uganda, forced women to become the breadwinners in their homes and consequently diluted the patriarchal nature of Ugandan society.

President Amin accelerated the weakening of patriarchy by declaring an economic war that culminated in expelling the Indian community from Uganda. Because this community had monopolised and dominated commerce, their departure left a vacuum. Ugandan males replaced the Indians. However, Amin, like many African dictators and quasi-dictators, became increasingly paranoid regarding potential competitors. Eventually, he forced all men considered to have money, including those who had taken over the Indian businesses, who might therefore pose a political threat, to quit their shops or face arrest and interrogation. This left the wives to operate the shop counters and eventually to manage the shops. Men's misfortune gave women an opportunity to take over and learn about commerce and trade. It also confirmed that women were capable of doing the same things as men, and doing them effectively.

The National Resistance Movement that ousted Obote II [5] further enhanced women's self-confidence by including women as resistance fighters. It also promoted women's emancipation by creating political structures that gave them a say in their lives. Specifically, special political positions were set aside for women from the village level to the national parliamentary level. At all levels, women are represented, either in the position of secretary for women or as members of the national parliament. Despite these gains, women in Uganda and elsewhere in Africa still endure more poverty, especially economic, than men (Bisi & Aina, 1995). Apparently, although the economic and political changes favourable to women's emancipation chipped away at patriarchy, they did little to change men's position in the hierarchy. We briefly examine Snyder's (2000) work to see how this has happened in Uganda. Table 2.10 describes the resilience of patriarchy despite events in Uganda and the world.

Snyder's study suggests that most women are locked permanently in subsistence agriculture or petty trade, although they manage to feed their children on a daily basis. While some women have managed to move from the burning sun to the boardroom, it is the majority, who do not, that concerns us. Her analysis reveals why women joined the market economy and became central actors in it and why men lost some of the power they held in the household. Nonetheless, the gender hierarchy that is part of African culture enabled men to retain much of their control of the home and its income. This culture defines men as the leaders in the home, while women manage it. Men's inability to provide for the home did not deprive them of leadership. Rather, they continued to lead and the women now had to use the money they earned to continue to manage the home. As a result, the money women made was consumed in the home and was not available for business expansion. One lesson of this analysis is that alleviating women's poverty will require interventions that identify the cultural values that underlie and justify treating women as less worthy than men. Examining the cultural profile in Uganda is a first step.

As noted in Table 2.4, women in Uganda are over-represented in crop farming, which is a poor source of income, and under-represented in other, more profitable income-producing activities. We next review a study by the Community Development

Table 2.8: Gender based obstacles in micro finance and micro enterprises

Obstacles	Individual	Household H/H	Wider community/national context
Financial	Women lack access to banks/finacial services in own right.	Men's control over cash income. Men's expenditure patterns.	Perception of men as controllers of money/loans. Inequitable distribution of resources from community and household activities in favour of men
Economic	Women undertake activities which produce low returns. Women have a heavy domestic workload.	Gender division of labour. Unequal access to and control of land, labour and inputs. Unequal control of joint household produce and income stream from this. Limited roles for women in H/H decision making	Women locked in low paid jobs Stereotypes of appropriate roles for women in the economy Women lack access to markets for inputs and outputs if mobility constrained due to social norms.
Social/Cultural	Women illiterate or uneducated; girls' education not priority.	Polygamy results in conflict / competition and discrimination between wives. Violence towards women.	Banks and financial institutions do not view women as a potential market Women's mobility constrained by social norms
Political/legal	Women lack confidence to claim political/legal rights.	Women lack legal rights to jointly owned h/h assets.	Women's legal rights to H/H assets not defined in law or useful for collateral Women lack political positions to establish appropriate laws Women lack legal rights to land both traditional and formal
Strategies to overcome constraints	Strategies which address women directly with awareness, literacy and related skills development.	Strategies directed to men in the community in order to affect men's behaviour towards women within the H/H and community.	Strategies aimed at affecting social norms and legal frameworks that might include advocacy work through the media and lobby to change women's rights to property.

Table 2.9: Dwindling patriarchy: An event listing matrix

Socio-historical phase/Author	Event 1	Event 2	Event 3	Event 4	Event 5
Colonial	Colonialists introduce cash economy.	They single out men as the central actors in the cash economy.	Men join paid employment and take responsibility for crop marketing.	Men gain or consolidate power over women.	Women are legally defined as minors.
International oil crisis of the 70s, Amin/Obote II in Uganda.	African economic crisis and Amin/Obote II in Uganda wipe out the real value of wages and salaries in Uganda.	Amin targets Uganda males, who 'disappear', are killed or go into hiding or exile.	• Peasant and middle class women replace Ugandan males in the market economy. • Women learn to manage businesses and to invest.	Exiled Ugandan women join the market economy (to supplement family income or as household head) and get investment and trading experience.	Uganda men's economic domination of women begins to crumble.

Socio-historical phase/ Author	Event 1	Event 2	Event 3	Event 4	Event 5
National Resistance Movement Government (NRM) and SAPS	NRM comes to power in Uganda. • Introduces affirmative action for Ugandan women. • Implements an economic recov ery programme (ERP/SAPS)	Women get representation quotas in local government and in the Parliament.	• ERP sets conditions. • Removes subsidies. • Down-sizes the traditional and non-traditional public service. • People lose jobs. • Cost of living soars.	• Retrenched women take to commerce and trade. • Women whose relatives or spouses have lost jobs take to commerce and trade to support families. • Women who are still employed are insecure against possible retrench ment and establish side incomes through trade and commerce.	Women establish themselves and are accepted as legitimate income generators in the family.

Table 2.10: The resilient patriarchy in Uganda: A dynamic event matrix

Triggering factor	Underlying cause	Coping mechanism	Solution	Outcome
Erosion of disposable real income in the family.	African economic/oil crisis of the 1970s	Moonlighting. Reduced outlays for family expenses.	Women join the market economy to supplement family income.	Weakening of men's economic domination of women.
Men's economic domination of women crumbles.	Amin targets Ugandan males who disappear, are killed or go into hiding/ exile.	Peasant and middle class women replace men in the market economy and learn to run businesses and to invest.	Women learn to become economically independent and men accept the changing role of women.	Men retain their hierarchical position as the de facto family head despite reduced economic contribution.
Women take responsibility for household expenses including children's health costs, school fees, etc.	Household management considered women's work.	Women join the market place to solve household basic needs.	Women's income becomes permanently locked in the household chores instead of reinvesting in business.	Peasant women permanently locked in petty trade.

Resource Network, (CDRN) and Dry Farmers' Resource Centre (DFRC) (1996) that examined how women fare in one of the more profitable activities, livestock production and management. This study shows that women have little opportunity to participate fully in livestock production and management. Generally, they are not allowed to own livestock or make decisions about its uses. Their main role was in providing labour – watering and feeding animals, overseeing small herds of grazing animals and processing livestock products. Because of their limited role, many women abandoned livestock products in favour of growing pulses and grains, leading to malnutrition in the family.

Figure 2.3 is a schematic summary of a large variety of documented events that we consider to be poverty carriers and indicators in Uganda, drawing on the Community

Figure 2.3: Poverty in Uganda: An historical, cultural and gender causal matrix

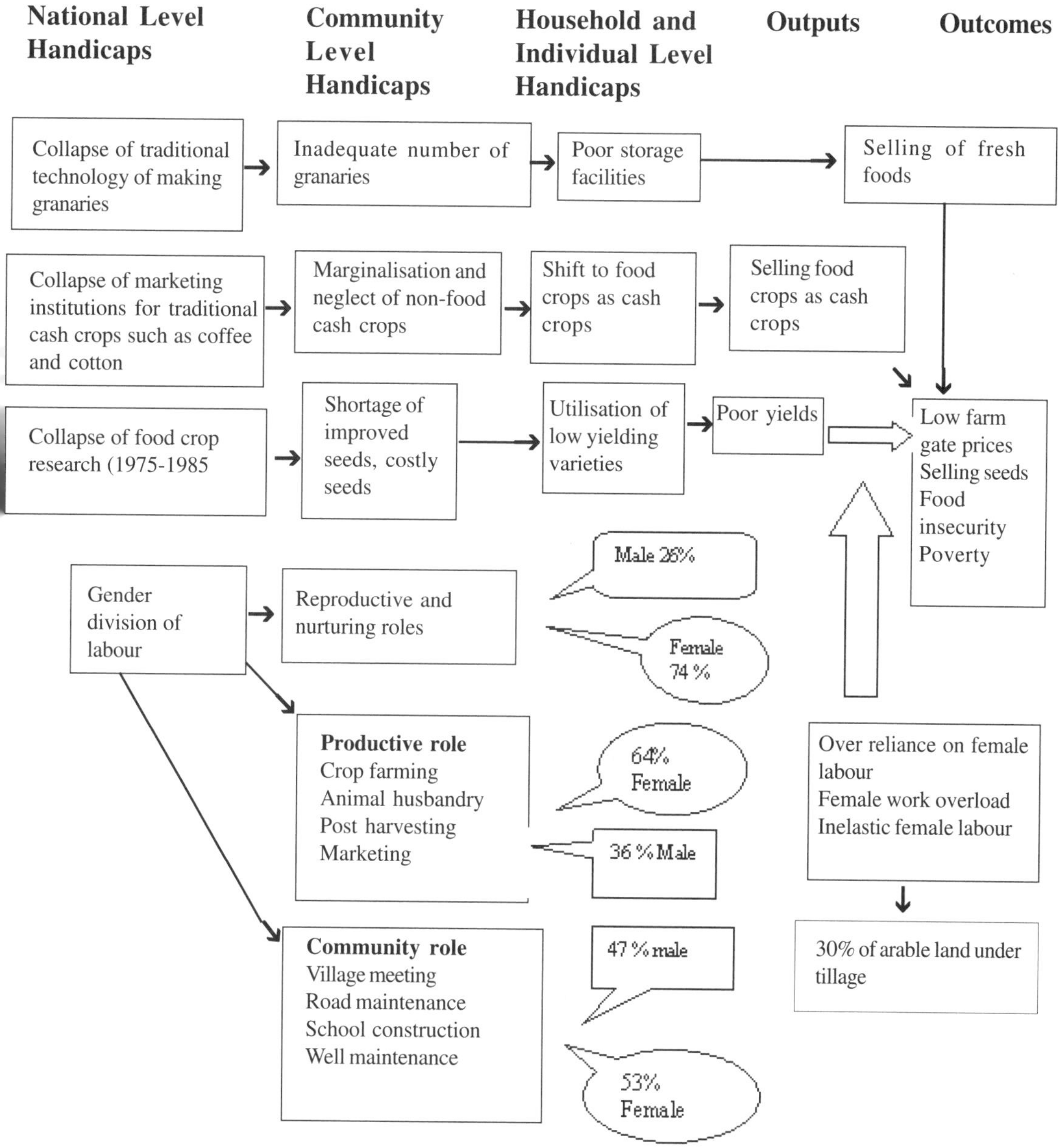

National Level Handicaps	Community Level Handicaps	Household and Individual Level Handicaps	Outputs	Outcomes

Collapse of traditional technology of making granaries → Inadequate number of granaries → Poor storage facilities → Selling of fresh foods

Collapse of marketing institutions for traditional cash crops such as coffee and cotton → Marginalisation and neglect of non-food cash crops → Shift to food crops as cash crops → Selling food crops as cash crops

Collapse of food crop research (1975-1985) → Shortage of improved seeds, costly seeds → Utilisation of low yielding varieties → Poor yields → Low farm gate prices Selling seeds Food insecurity Poverty

Gender division of labour → Reproductive and nurturing roles

Male 26%

Female 74 %

Productive role
Crop farming
Animal husbandry
Post harvesting
Marketing

64% Female

36 % Male

Over reliance on female labour
Female work overload
Inelastic female labour

Community role
Village meeting
Road maintenance
School construction
Well maintenance

47 % male

53% Female

30% of arable land under tillage

Development Resource Network, and Dry Farmers' Resource Centre (1996). The initial causal events are described as handicaps found at the national, community, and household/individual levels. The bottom half of the figure leaves little doubt that the distribution of gender roles is closely associated with poverty.

Figure 2.3 emphasises the association between continued poverty in Uganda and culture-determined gender roles. It leads to the conclusion that continued engineering of gender rights may not adequately address the underlying problem; it will also be necessary to modify the values that perpetuate and justify the gender distribution of labour. As background for further consideration of gender and poverty, we summarise, in Table 2.11 the main aspects of gender inequality in Uganda. We also note the main reasons put forward for changing gender roles and some of the methods that have been proposed to accomplish this.

The indicators of inequality in the first column of Table 2.11 are also carriers of poverty. Many of these are steeped in cultural values. An example is the customary laws, which pose structural barriers to full female participation in income generating activities. The customary law of inheritance, for instance, prohibits girl children and wives from inheriting land from their fathers or their husbands respectively. This deprives them of an easy and institutionalised way to preserve a major productive resource in a subsistence economy. It binds them to their male relatives or relatives-in-law. Other examples are the early age of marriage, submission to men's sexual demands, and denial of participation in home decision-making. To deal with value-related barriers to equality, the types of proposals listed in the last column will not suffice. Rather, the values that justify each type of inequality may have to be identified, made explicit, and examined jointly with the community, in search of alternative value preferences.

Poverty indicators and carriers in the current study

The current study investigated efforts to alleviate poverty in seven districts of Uganda (See Chapter 1). In this section, we describe in more detail the samples studied, their levels of literacy, household expenditures on food and non-consumables, and expenditures on income-generating activities. The samples consisted of men and women who had joined self-help projects (project group) and those who had not joined such projects (control group). The project group (n=293) consisted largely of those we could conveniently reach as well as those who were pointed out to us or to our researchers by project co-ordinators. The sampling effort for the project group targeted women more than men because women are more vulnerable to poverty. Moreover, poverty alleviation programmes have also targeted them. We selected a control group (n = 108) of household heads who had joined no project and who lived two houses away from a project member in the study. We gathered data with an in-depth interview that lasted approximately three hours. Most interviews were done by graduate researchers who met respondents at their place of work, including in the gardens of those who were farmers. Respondents answered most questions, but there was the expected reluctance to answer questions regarding income. Table 2.12 presents the numbers of participants in the control and project samples in each district. As can be seen, the largest samples came from the Central region, with smaller samples from both the Northern and Western regions.

Table 2.13 presents the distribution of the samples by district and gender. Data on gender was missing for four participants. The majority of respondents were female in all but the Northern region. The predominance of males in the Northern region probably reflects the insecurity in the region. Rapes and abductions of young girls and women were common in the region at the time of interviewing, so women were less willing to meet our interviewer and generally did not venture out of safe places unless the reason for doing so was essential.

Table 2.11: Gender inequality in Uganda and how to address it

Indicators of inequality	Roles of women	Reasons why gender roles should change	Proposed ways to change gender roles
• Women work longer hours than men. • Women have more limited access to resources. • Women have more limited access to power, politics, the law, etc. • Some laws, i.e. customary laws, still discriminate against women. • Women have no control over what they produce. • Women do not participate in decision-making in the home. • Women marry at an early age. • Women submit to men's sexual demands. • Women are more vulnerable to sexually transmitted diseases.	• Household worker • Health care in the homes • Water and sanitation • Child-bearing and caring • Fetching water and firewood • Home education/ socialisation/ counselling • Provider of food for the family • Custodian of culture • Looking after domestic animals • Digging/garden preparing	• To create gender balance and equity. • To bring about equality between men and women. • To promote the socio-economic status of the family. • To relieve women of the burden of work especially of being responsible for food production for the whole family. • Because allocation of gender roles was wrongly based on culture and cutoms that are oppressive to women.	• Through gender sensitisation of families, communities, and political leaders. • Involving men and women in socio-economic and political activities. • Devising means of providing appropriate technology to reduce women's workload.

Table 2.12: Target sample size by district

Region	District	Control group	Project group	Total
Western	Bushenyi	15	24	39
	Kabale	9	24	33
Northern	Arua	10	22	32
	Nebbi	18	29	47
Central	Mukono	23	75	98
	Masaka	24	80	104
	Mpigi	9	39	48
	Total	108	293	401

Table 2.13: Target sample size by district by sex

Regions	Districts	Male	Females	Total
Western	Bushenyi	24	15	39
	Kabale	4	29	33
Northern	Arua	18	13	31
	Nebbi	29	18	47
Central	Mukono	35	60	95
	Masaka	19	85	104
	Mpigi	5	43	48
Total		134	236	397

Table 2.14: Literacy status of the study sample

Regions	District	Percentage literate	
		Male	Female
Western	Bushenyi	100 % (24)	93 % (14)
	Kabale	100 % (4)	53 % (17)
Northern	Arua	94 % (17)	92 % (12)
	Nebbi	82 % (24)	78 % (14)
Central	Mukono	97 % (34)	100 % (60)
	Masaka	100 % (19)	97 % (82)
	Mpigi	100 % (5)	42 % (98)

Table 2.15: Expenditures in the study sample by sex

Type of expenditure	Sex	N	Mean	T	df	Sig.
General household inputs such as saucepans	Male	97	1.89	3.08	301	0.002
	Female	206	1.38			
General business inputs such as perishable agricultural petty trade items	Male	78	1.39	2.57	264	0.01
	Female	188	0.96			
Luxury items e.g. video deck and refrigerator	Male	113	0.24	1.89	339	0.058
	Female	228	0.15			
Costly business inputs such as land	Male	79	0.74	2.59	266	0.01
	Female	189	0.47			

Table 2.14 reveals that literacy levels in the study sample. This indicator of poverty was similar to the literacy trends for the whole country.

On the whole, literacy was somewhat higher among the men in the samples than among the women, as is typical in Uganda. However, as a group, the women in these samples were more educated than women in the national statistics. This was probably because more educated women were more likely to be involved in development projects, and these were the women we interviewed.

We also examined gender differences in various types of expenditure. These included general household items such as cups and saucepans and luxury items such as video decks and refrigerators. The other types of expenditure were business inputs of the general and relatively costly type. Agricultural chemicals and land exemplified the relatively costly inputs. The general inputs were instanced by restocking of petty trade items such as perishable and non-perishable agricultural produce. A list of these items was read to the respondents who answered whether or not they had purchased each item (scored 1 or 0). Table 2.15 shows that men spent more than women on every one of the types of expenditure. This gender difference is congruent with the national statistics on gender differences in wealth.

Conclusion

This chapter has provided an overview of poverty in Africa, emphasising the Ugandan experience. We have paid particular attention to gender differences in poverty and to the ways individual poor people themselves experience and perceive poverty. In our qualitative analysis we have tried to focus on the social psychological individual to draw attention to the importance of understanding the life experiences and actions of the individual person who copes with poverty as the basis of policy formulation. We recommended that researchers and policy-makers closely observe and listen to these individuals, who are found in the streets trying to hawk their wares, selling cooked food, sitting in crowded markets, and walking to their places of work.

We use the label 'social psychological individual' in order to emphasise the need to understand how the poor interact continuously with others, deliberately forming and drawing upon social networks to ensure their own survival. Among the other deliberate actions of the poor that must be understood are the short-term tactical decisions they make and the longer-term strategies they employ to preserve their limited resources or improve their situation. We have identified some of the poverty carriers, the acts that perpetuate or produce poverty, acts that must change if individuals are to escape poverty. We have suggested that, in order to develop successful methods for alleviating poverty, it is necessary to uncover the specific acts in the daily lives of the poor that lead to poverty. If these poverty-carrying acts are identified, academics and practitioners can more easily design policies to target them directly.

Our data set reproduced the gendered poverty profile that the national statistics demonstrate: men consistently outspend women in the study sample. We also explored in some detail how women are kept in a position of poverty relative to men. We observed that the consistency of this phenomenon suggests an underlying cultural pattern of values that supports this way of treating women and men. The search for the underlying cultural pattern of motivational values, of which this study is a part, is timely because, as the literature indicates, gender relations are associated with poverty in Uganda. The next chapter examines the meaning of culture from the point of view of cultural values.

––––––––––––––––––––––––––––––

1. Uganda Bureau of Statistics (1997)

2. Mr Muwonge, Senior Principal Statistician, Uganda Bureau of Statistics. Personal communication.

3. In Chapter 6 we will discuss the advantages to a community of migrants with resources and leverage.

4. The Government of Uganda with help from the World Food Programme instituted the Heifer Project for Women Farmers (HPWF) where women farmers obtained in-calf exotic cows to rent on a zero grazing system (grazing from a shaded cubicle). The objectives of the project were to assist beneficiaries in rural and peri-urban areas become socially and economically self-reliant, to supplement family income through milk sales, to provide a constant supply of milk to the household and their neighbours and to increase dairy herds depleted during the wars (Matovu, 1995, p1).

5. Obote II refers to Milton Obote's second term as president of Uganda, widely seen as illegal and destructive. His regime was toppled by General Tito Okello Lutwa in July 1985.

3

Culture, Cultural Interface
and Development in Africa

In this chapter, we discuss culture as a necessary though insufficient condition for development. We distinguish between weak and strong cultures (Gyekye, 1997). We examine culture as the context in which growth and development take place and discuss African culture and modernity, starting from an African philosophical anthropology framework. We present a model of cultural values to illustrate the meaning and importance of culture as a source of motivation, expressed in values at both the community and individual levels. We finally introduce the concept of the cultural interface to emphasise the point that the operative culture in Africa is mainly defined by the recent intensive cultural contact between colonising and host cultures (Nsamenang & Dawes, 1998). We provide examples of negative and positive cultural interfaces as behavioural manifestations of underlying cultural values.

Weak and strong cultures: The meaning of culture

The production of written documents on African cultures was pioneered by social and cultural anthropologists, who still dominate this field. The strength of social and cultural anthropology models lies in their focus on the uniqueness of each unit of study such as a village, an ethnic group, or a nation. This approach has provided deep insights into each of the African cultural units studied, for example, the Basoga of Uganda (Fallers, 1965). However, it rarely seeks what is common to the units studied, thereby giving the impression that each Black African nation and its sub-cultures are unique (Gyekye, 1987). Nevertheless, most Africans will see reflections of their daily experience in literature-from fiction to organisational studies- from widely separated regions of Africa, such as Marris[1] (1968) description of African entrepreneurs in North Africa and Chinua Achebe's (1958) *Things Fall Apart* from West Africa. Moreover, the significant migrations from Southern to Eastern Africa and vice versa (Ssekamwa, 1984) in pre-colonial Africa make the existence of similarities across African cultures likely. These migrations may explain the presence of a Bantu linguistic belt stretching from Tanzania, Kenya, and Uganda in East Africa, to some of the Zulu tribes of South Africa.

Because the dominant anthropological model does not focus on similarities across Africa, we must look elsewhere for enlightenment on the widely perceived cultural kinship among Africans. For this we turn to African philosophical anthropologists who have long sought to show and explain how and why Africans are culturally related (see, for instance, Mbiti, 1969). The following discussion is centrally informed by Gyekye's recent works on *African Philosophical Thought* (Gyekye, 1995) and especially on his *Tradition and Modernity* (Gyekye, 1997).

Gyekye distinguishes between strong and weak cultures. He says: 'The strong sense [implies] that in literally all aspects of their cultural life, people in a given cultural environment live the same way; eat the same food, wear the same clothing, share the same tastes, have common political, religious, and moral beliefs, think, act, and react in the same way...' (1997: 112). This, he claims, is an idealistic and impractical conception of culture, because no peoples lead such a unified cultural life. Instead, he proposes a weak view of culture that refers to a cultural community when a people share some significant, identifiable, values and practices. This view avoids a monolithic conception of cultural life and instead allows for the expression of individual or group tastes, sentiments, preferences, and ways of responding to local or particular experiences (Gyekye, 1997:113). Moreover, it is only in the weak sense that we can legitimately speak of national cultures such as American or British cultures. The weak cultures concept makes it possible to look for and appreciate similarities between peoples, and to identify larger rather than smaller cultural communities. Adopting the weak view of culture makes it plausible for Africans to think of themselves as culturally related.

Culture as the context for learning, development and growth

A link between culture and development is now widely recognised. It has led to a sustained effort to integrate culture into development policies (Accra Conference, 1975; UNESCO, 1982; 1995; World Bank (Serageldin & Taboroff, 1994; CIDA, 1995; OAU, undated). Despite this effort, little progress has been made and little is known about relevant cultural facts and how they impact on development (Diagne & Ossebi, 1996). One problem is that culture has come to mean everything and nothing (Diagne & Ossebi, 1996; Bloom, 1987). UNESCO's (1982) working definition exemplifies the problem. It reads:

> Culture is a ...set of distinctive, spiritual, material, intellectual and emotional features that characterise a society or a social group. Other than arts and humanities, it covers modes of life, fundamental human rights, value systems, traditions and beliefs.

The comprehensiveness of this definition is its undoing. Sceptics dismiss it as too global to permit systematic conceptualisation (Gilbert, 1989). They prefer a more common sense approach that focuses on more tangible ecological, sociological or cultural variables (Segall, 1984). The problem with this alternative approach is the sheer number of potentially relevant variables and the absence of a theory for understanding their interrelations, organising them, and choosing among them (Jahoda, 1984; Gilbert, 1989). Even if one succeeds in identifying relevant cultural or ecological units, the processes through which societal or community change occurs must be made clear. By understanding these processes, we can begin to see the relationship between culture and development and systematically create opportunities for integrating culture into development policy.

We adopt the action view of culture as the context within which development takes place or, as Diagne & Ossebi (1996) say, the context within which new ideas, such as the market economy and technology, must be negotiated. This view sees culture as a set of control mechanisms such as plans, recipes and instructions governing behaviour (Geertz, 1975). Culture provides the tools and the environment for learning how to function in society (Vygotsky, 1978, Geertz, 1975; Gilbert, 1989), the how and the why (Hofstede, 1992). People reproduce their culture as they learn how to function, and they transform their culture as they learn why they should function in particular ways (Gilbert, 1989).

Cultural and cross-cultural psychologists have focused on the value system of a society as an important mediating tool of human mental functioning (Vygotsky, 1978, Hofstede, 1992, Schwartz, 1992). Values are trans-situational goals that vary in importance and serve as guiding principles in life (Rokeach, 1973; Schwartz, 1992). At the individual level, values are the goals that direct, energise and serve to justify a person's behaviour. Values help to account for individual differences in attitudes and behaviour. Individuals acquire their values through interaction with others to satisfy their needs and pursue their goals. Subsequently they use values as tools to persuade others and win their co-operation and co-ordination in pursuing personal and joint goals.

At the culture level, values are shared goals. Groups that have a common bond, such as nations and religious and ethnic groups, draw upon shared cultural values to generate standards and ideals for regulating the ways they handle the challenges of life and reproduce themselves. Cultural values are called upon to justify the working rules and assumptions of a group. Thus cultural values are expressed in the ways that societal institutions function and in the justifications that societal leaders and members provide for their behaviour (Schwartz, 1994a, 2004).

Cultural value priorities also affect the way social resources are allocated (Schwartz 2004). The relative importance attributed to such values as wealth, justice and beauty partly determines how money, land, and human capital are allocated and deployed in a society. Are they invested more in industrialisation (expressing a value emphasis on wealth), social welfare (justice), or preserving the environment (beauty)? Cultural value priorities also determine how organisational performance is evaluated. In a culture where creativity and change are highly valued, for example, employee innovation may elicit praise and material reward, even if the innovation alters established practices and hierarchical role relations. The same innovative performance might be condemned in a culture that emphasises the maintenance of authority and stability.

Two major lines of current research have sought to identify a comprehensive set of cultural value dimensions. Hofstede (1980, 1992) suggested that five cultural value dimensions could be derived from the ways societal members typically cope with core societal problems. He called these dimensions Power Distance, Individualism/ Collectivism, Uncertainty Avoidance, Masculinity/Femininity, and Short/Long Time Orientation. While widely employed, the Hofstede dimensions have been subject to many serious criticisms (e.g., Kagitcibasi, 1997; McSweeney, 2001, Schwartz, 1997). Hofstede also provided little data on sub-Saharan Africa. This book utilises a more recent set of cultural values suggested by Schwartz (1994, 1999, 2004; Schwartz & Ross, 1995) for which there are data from five black African nations. We explicate these seven cultural value orientations below. Schwartz derived these orientations by identifying three basic social issues with which societies must cope. The different cultural adaptations that evolve to resolve each of these issues form three bipolar cultural dimensions.

Embeddedness versus Autonomy.[2] This dimension concerns the relationship between individual and group, the extent to which persons are seen as autonomous entities versus embedded parts of groups. Cultures that emphasise embeddedness values (e.g., social order, respect for tradition, family security, and self-discipline) stress maintenance of the status quo, propriety, and restraint of actions or inclinations that might disrupt group solidarity and the traditional order. In these cultures, people seek meaning in life largely through social relationships, through identifying with the group in which they are embedded and participating in its shared way of life (cf. Markus & Kitayama, 1991, on cultures with an interdependent construal of self). Recent literature on social capital suggests that societal features (referred to as 'bonding') inherent in embeddedness are crucial in attracting individuals back to their communities and inducing them to invest in long-term projects and to forego short-term for long-term gains (Putnam, 1993; Temkin & Rohe 1998).

In high autonomy cultures, the person is viewed as an autonomous, bounded entity who finds meaning in his or her own uniqueness, who seeks to express his or her own internal attributes (preferences, traits, feelings, motives) and is encouraged to do so. Two related types of autonomy are distinguished. Intellectual Autonomy emphasises the independent ideas and rights of the individual to pursue his/her own intellectual directions (exemplary values: curiosity, broadmindedness, creativity). Affective Autonomy emphasises the individual's independent pursuit of affectively positive experience (pleasure, exciting life, and varied life).

Hierarchy versus Egalitarianism. This dimension concerns assuring responsible social behaviour, motivating people to consider others' welfare and to co-ordinate with them in order to manage their unavoidable interdependencies. In high hierarchy cultures, a hierarchical system of ascribed roles ensures socially responsible behaviour. Hierarchy values emphasise the legitimacy of an unequal distribution of power, roles and resources (social power, authority, humility, and wealth). People are socialised and sanctioned to comply with the obligations and rules attached to their roles. High Egalitarianism cultures portray individuals as moral equals who share basic interests as human beings. People are socialised to internalise a commitment to voluntary co-operation with others and to feel concern for everyone's welfare. Egalitarianism values emphasise transcendence of selfish interests (equality, social justice, freedom, responsibility, and honesty). They are a focus of socialisation in cultures where the person is viewed as autonomous rather than interdependent, because autonomous persons have no natural commitment to others.

Mastery versus Harmony. This dimension concerns the place of humankind in the natural and social world: is humankind's role more to submit, to fit in, or to exploit? In high Mastery cultures, people actively seek to master and change the natural and social world, to assert control, bend it to their will, and exploit it in order to further personal or group interests. Mastery values emphasise getting ahead through active self-assertion (ambition, success, daring, and competence). High Harmony cultures accept the world as it is, trying to preserve rather than to change or exploit it. Harmony values emphasise fitting harmoniously into the environment (world at peace, unity with nature, world of beauty). Fatalism as a way of life is the extreme form of this cultural orientation, a submissive adaptation uncommon in contemporary societies, but not unknown (Douglas, 1982; Wildavsky, 1992). The balance of Mastery and Harmony values in a culture is especially relevant because it affects whether productive activity is organised in an activist, exploitative and competitive way or in a way that is harmonious, socially responsible and co-operative.

Cultural interfaces as a consequence of globalisation

Attempts to characterise the world's societies from economic and political perspectives have yielded simplified dichotomies such as rich and poor nations, North and South, East and West, communist and democratic, etc. Theories and research on cultural dimensions reveal that many of these economic and political dichotomies are indeed associated with distinctive cultural profiles (Hofstede, 1980; Inglehart, 1999; Schwartz, 1999, 2004). However, these theories emphasise that, whatever the unit of analysis, whether nations, larger geographic regions, or sub-cultures within societies, the cultural profile of each unit describes its position in relation to numerous value dimensions rather than as part of a particular sharply defined political or economic group. This dimensional approach enables theory and research to take into account the potential impacts on culture of the complex changes associated with globalisation.

Globalisation entails an intensive, significant, and continuous interaction among societies. Presumably, it alters local structures, defences, and identities (Wilkinson, 1995). By examining cultural change on a variety of dimensions empirically, we can uncover the dimensions on which shifts in culture traceable to globalisation occur and the magnitude of such shifts. We can determine the extent to which political and economic boundaries correspond to cultural boundaries and, if not, how previously uniform cultures are splitting or recombining into new ones. As members of different cultural units come into contact, they try to work out ways to co-ordinate, and they may experience conflict and change. To examine this process more closely, we draw upon the concept of the cultural interface (Munene, 1999, Munene & Isingoma, 2000).

An interface is an abstraction that refers to the interpersonal or inter-group space generated when different groups or cultures meet in the process of a social or economic transaction. Unlike a contact point that is more or less a finite point in space, an interface is an ongoing process characterising the way the parties (agents) relate to each other. It is the joint, interactional outcome of the motivations, values, beliefs, perceptions, and underlying experiences that each party brings to the exchange. The cultural interface construct can be fruitfully applied for relating culture to development. When people from groups that differ in their culturally approved patterns of behaviour come into contact (for example, around a task such as making an investment), the resulting cultural interface may be one of conflict or congruence (Fallers, 1965). Congruence ensues when actors have complementary and compatible expectations (Parsons, T. 1951, from Fallers, 1965) leading to positive interdependence. The meshing of complementary expectations is the ideal cultural interface where individuals and groups are able to recognise their interdependence and to be mutually supportive of one another.

Conflict, the alternative outcome of culture contact, occurs when people in a situation of interdependence hold contradictory expectations, so their behaviour is mutually incompatible.[3] We term the conflict *exogenous* when one or more of the interacting parties behaves according to culturally approved expectations from outside the host culture. It is *endogenous* when both parties are from within the same society. This conflictual cultural interface frequently takes the form of role conflict–personal or organisational strain caused when incompatible expectations from different roles are focused upon the same actor.

Role conflict is widespread in Africa. It is the most researched cultural interface (see Blunt, 1983). Fallers (1965) found that role conflict brought about political and social discontinuities in his Ugandan samples. The difficulty of working in modern institutions that demand loyalty on the basis of role incumbency caused the strains. Typical Ugandans felt obligated to express loyalty in the traditional manner of conforming to the individuals in authority, not to role incumbents. Other African researchers who have studied the role conflict cultural interface have identified such consequences as social disequilibrium, disharmonious discontinuities, intrapersonal conflict or strain and instability in institutions, nepotism, and corruption (Price, 1975; Magid, 1976). Fallers (1965) attributes the prevalence of role conflict in Africa to the extensive influence of the institution of kinship within bureaucracies and to a failure to create counter-institutions such as rules to govern conflicts of interest that might exclude this influence.

The conflict inherent in contact among cultures in Africa is also an opportunity cost of development that we must understand better. For this purpose, we must closely examine how the cultural context in which behaviour is embedded influences the ways people carry out their own culturally conditioned actions in the course of exchanging resources and information (cf. Granovetter, 1985). Only a close study of this cultural interface can lead to the control and management of culturally based role-conflict (cf. Fallers, 1965).

In theory, interactions between any two people with different cultural expectations constitute a unique cultural interface. Here, we focus on the cultural interface that emerges when the interacting parties come from substantially different cultures. We also consider the type of cultural interface that emerges when people try to carry out tasks outside their cultural experience. This occurs when the cultural tools they are familiar with, such as language, values and technology, are inadequate for undertaking or completing a task. Later, we elaborate on familiar African cultural interfaces associated with gender roles (Afonja and Aina, 1995) and with the 'economy of affection' (Hyden, 1983).[4] First, we present a recent study that examined how cultural differences in prevailing national values create problems when Africans and change agents from non-African nations work together (Munene, Schwartz, and Smith, 2000).

Implications of national values for the cultural interface of donor-host contacts in Africa

Munene et al. (2000) demonstrate empirically that several black African nations share a common cultural value profile (see also later in Chapter 4) and that most donor nations share a different cultural value profile. They analyse how the cultural value priorities that guide the behaviours and influence the decision-making practices of the typical manager in each set of nations are diametrically opposed. Table 3.1 sums up their view of what regularly occurs when representatives from donor and host nations meet in Africa to initiate and implement development programmes, including national budgets.

Table 3.1 highlights the lack of fit between the cultural values and practices of the Africans and West Europeans, between what they are predisposed to justify and to sanction. Culturally, samples from the African countries endorsed hierarchy, embeddedness and mastery values but gave little legitimacy to autonomy, egalitarianism

Table 3.1 Cultural values underlying cultural interfaces between Africans and West Europeans

Cultural Groups	Institution			
	Predisposed to defend and justify		Predisposed to delegitimise and sanction	
	Cultural values	Cultural practices	Cultural values	Cultural practices
Africans	Embeddedness Hierarchy Mastery	Turning to own experience and to subordinates to interpret events	Intellectual Autonomy Affective Autonomy Egalitarianism Harmony	Turning to formal rules and deferring to superiors to interpret events
West Europeans	Intellectual Autonomy Affective Autonomy Egalitarianism Harmony	Turning to formal rules and deferring to superiors to interpret events	Embeddedness Hierarchy Mastery	Turning to own experience and to subordinates to interpret events

and harmony values. This means that people in these countries find behaviour compatible with the first set of values justified and even desirable and behaviour compatible with the second less legitimate and even undesirable. In contrast, the samples from European countries endorsed the opposite set of values--intellectual and affective autonomy, egalitarianism and harmony values, and they gave little legitimacy to embeddedness, hierarchy and mastery. Thus the pattern of value priorities in the African and European samples constituted a sharp mismatch. Many African workers and Europeans who work in Africa experience this kind of mismatch every day in a variety of ways.

Table 3.1 illustrates some of the ways the conflicting value orientations affect everyday decision making. Their cultural background inclines African managers to prefer drawing on their bosses or superiors and on formal rules when reaching decisions. The cultural background of European managers inclines them to rely more on their own experiences and to turn more to their subordinates for advice. These different ways of reaching decisions make it likely that the cultural interface that characterises transactions in projects sponsored by Western donor agencies in Africa will be filled with conflict. This may partly explain the disappointing outcomes of many donor driven projects that populate the economic landscape of sub-Saharan Africa. Such projects, as noted in Chapter 1, have not borne the fruits they were meant to bear. Many have failed, leaving the Africans on the African continent as poor as or poorer than before.

The economies of Uganda and of almost all other sub-Saharan African countries (excepting Botswana and, to a degree, Mauritius) are predominantly capitalised by donor nations that were included in the Munene, et al. study. Note that the African host nations and the West European donor nations have cultures that predispose their citizens to justify or reject not only different values but contradictory values! Thus the cultural interface that emerges in working together can be expected to produce psychological and personal tension that may lead to organisational instability. It is therefore unlikely that genuine dialogue is possible without deliberate efforts on both sides to face their cultural differences. The lack of sustainability of many projects that donors initiate and the relatively low productivity of local counterparts (Munene, 1995) illustrate the effects of such cultural conflict.

The analysis in Table 3.1 demonstrates the importance of searching for the relevant culturally patterned behaviours that underlie each cross-cultural transaction, as recommended years ago by Fallers (1965), recently by Hofstede (1992), and more recently by Trompenaars and Hampden-Turner (1998). Donor and host nations have tried to evade the problem of cultural incompatibility by introducing more participatory processes. But participation has different connotations and significance for different people (see Chapter 6). It is no substitute for uncovering the problematic cultural interfaces that may be wreaking havoc with African attempts to move out of poverty. The tension and organisational instability implied by Table 3.1 is clearly demonstrated in a job evaluation exercise, sponsored by the World Bank in an effort to revitalise the Ugandan public service, that we discuss next.

Applying the equity principle in an institutional reform programme in Uganda: A problematic cultural interface

From 1993 through 2000, the Uganda public service undertook a comprehensive reform programme (Public Service Reform Programme /PSRP) composed of several measures for improving efficiency and effectiveness. The reform was articulated in a vision statement, labelled 'The Public Service We Need at a Price We Can Afford', and a twin strategy of Result Oriented Management (ROM) and Output Oriented Budgeting (OOB). As part of carrying out this strategy, ministries and departments were downsized from 32 to 22. Public service staff was reduced from 320,000 to 92,000. A job evaluation exercise, completed in 1996, recommended new job grades and a revised salary structure. However, by 1997, the public service had rejected both reports. Moreover, it had persuaded the consortium of donors, including the World Bank, to fund new ministerial restructuring and job re-evaluation exercises. The results of these new exercises are unlikely to be more successful. Individual ministries, such as Health, were structured a third time, and the new job grades completed before 1998 had still not been implemented by 2001.

The first, abortive attempt to structure job grades illustrates how a non-accommodative national culture frustrates the acceptance and implementation of innovations. The first step in job grading is to identify and agree upon a set of criteria or factors to be used in evaluating the importance of jobs. Such factors might include necessary education, experience, and responsibility for staff, for example. These factors can serve as a basis for determining a job holder's monetary compensation, that is, they are 'compensatable'. Each organisation then decides upon the relative importance to the organisation of each of the compensatable factors. Thus, one organisation may assign equal value to experience and education while another rates one or the other more important.

Each organisation may identify as many factors as it considers relevant. The more factors an organisation specifies, the more finely it can discriminate among jobs. An organisation that evaluates jobs based only on education and experience will classify many jobs as equally important, for example, university professor and consultant surgeon. If the same organisation also considers risk a compensatable factor, the riskier job of consultant surgeon would earn a higher grade than the job of university professor.

The process of selecting and weighting compensatable factors is obviously value-ridden. Careful job analysis and competence profiling can introduce greater transparency to the process, but values must still be applied after this is done. Values, and the principles that express them, also determine the final outcome of job grading and compensation even after the importance of each job has been classified. One principle is equity: jobs should be assigned grades precisely in proportion to their level of difficulty expressed by a given weight. Another principle is parity or equality: jobs that carry the same title or status should receive the same grade, even if they have different weights.

The 1996 job evaluation and grading exercise was the fifth in the life of the Ugandan public service. The first three exercises, carried out in 1955, 1961, and 1976, had all used and upheld the principle of equity. In practical terms, this meant two things:

1.　Jobholders carrying the same job title were paid more or less according to the number and burden of their tasks and the weight of their responsibilities.
2.　Jobholders who had greater burdens and responsibilities than their administrative superiors were paid more than their superiors.

The earlier compensation schemes aroused little disgruntlement for two reasons. First, they used education and experience as the only compensatable factors. This led to classifying many jobs as equivalent and masking the consequences of the equity principle. Second, fringe benefits were added to positions of higher status, undermining the impact on income of using the equity principle in grading jobs. This maintained the traditional hierarchy of jobs.

In the 1982 job evaluation and grading exercise, decision-making responsibility was introduced as a third factor for weighting job importance. This change led to finer discrimination among jobs and sharpened the consequences of applying the equity principle. For example, directors with different amounts of decision-making responsibility might receive different grades. The commission that conducted the 1982 job evaluation chose to apply the equity principle between but not within grades. Within grades, the equality principle applied. Thus, permanent secretaries in all ministries received the same remuneration, despite variations in what they were required to do in the different ministries. In this way, permanent secretaries always received larger salaries than commissioners who were their subordinates, even if the permanent secretaries had less responsibility than the commissioners. This was more acceptable because it respected the cultural expectation of hierarchy.

The 1996 job evaluation and job grading exercise increased the number of compensatable factors to ten: education, experience, physical effort, mental effort, responsibility for staff, responsibility for getting along with others, responsibility for confidential matters, responsibility for the consequences of error, working environment, responsibility for assets/money. This greatly enhanced discrimination among jobs and radically upset the status quo. Applying the equity principle to compensate the highly discriminated classes of jobs differentially strongly defied cultural expectations of hierarchy. Four outcomes of doing so proved particularly contentious. First, the grades and salaries given to permanent secretaries[5] and commissioners varied according to the ministry in which they were located. Second, some subordinate positions received higher grades and remuneration than supervisory positions. Third, policies that protected the positions of high-ranking administrators were changed, making them vulnerable. For instance, it became possible to transfer permanent secretaries from higher paying to lower paying jobs, threatening jobholders' careers, livelihood and status. Finally, the weight of experience in determining job grades was increased relative to that of education, so that public servants without university diplomas or qualifications could be graded in the same category or higher than those with university degrees.

The upsetting impact of the new system of job grading was exacerbated because the Uganda public service had earlier stopped the practice of using fringe benefits to reward status. Fringe benefits could no longer make up for lower salaries, so higher status jobs that received less compensation truly experienced the effects of applying the equity principle. Despite widespread agreement that the equity principle was fair, the four consequences of applying the principle, noted above, were not accepted. Consequently, the service rejected the report, wasting the approximately $562,000 invested by the state to produce it. This decision made no sense in terms of simple rationality. However, it made good cultural sense considering the cultural interface that was the context of the decision. Most relevant is the prevailing cultural commitment to hierarchy. Uganda ranked third among 54 nations on a cultural index of hierarchy values developed by Schwartz (1999; see Munene, Schwartz,& Smith, 2000). In a hierarchical culture, societal members view the allocation of influence, resources, status, and wealth to hierarchically ordered positions as the legitimate and desirable way to organise relations among people and to induce people to work for the greater good. The smooth functioning of society depends upon maintaining a hierarchical order of ascribed positions in which people accept authority from above them and exercise authority over those below them. On the cultural hierarchy index, Uganda, Zimbabwe, Nigeria and Ghana respectively occupied ranks 3, 8, 14, and 18, among 54 nations.

The importance of hierarchy in the dominant culture in Uganda makes clear why the results of the sophisticated, rational job evaluation had to be rejected. In a hierarchical culture, resources are legitimately allocated according to ascribed positions in the hierarchy. Compensating job holders on the basis of objective factors reflecting the levels of difficulty and responsibility of their jobs, while ignoring their hierarchical position, is illegitimate. It contradicts basic, taken-for-granted assumptions about how society should be organised. Such an approach would be more acceptable in cultures that emphasise egalitarianism as the principle on which to allocate resources, cultures that attribute little importance to hierarchy, such as Denmark (Schwartz, 1999).

In sum, the fundamental decisions made by administrators and managers of organisations and national economies reflect the cultural interface that serves as their context. Seen from the perspective of this context, decisions like the rejection of the 1996 job grading exercise in Uganda are logical, since, Ugandans are culturally predisposed to defend hierarchy and to reject egalitarianism. Taken out of their cultural context, such decisions appear to be illogical.

Gender roles as sources of problematic cultural interfaces

We briefly comment on how contact between men and women produces problematic cultural interfaces due to the different cultural expectations of males and females in Uganda and related African cultures. For example, it is normal practice for male business partners and potential partners to go out together late at night with the expectation of hatching new business opportunities. For a married businesswoman to engage in this practice is against the cultural norm, however. She will encounter strong societal disapproval and create marital problems for herself. If she refrains from or discontinues the practice, she will lose out on business opportunities. Thus, she finds herself in a costly cultural interface due to gender roles.

Figure 2.3 in Chapter 2 identified a variety of costly conditions associated with the gender role cultural interface that lead to food insecurity in Uganda. In combination, cultural commitments to hierarchy and to patriarchy serve to handicap food production in rural areas. Hierarchy justifies granting the right to determine what happens in the community to those in authority. Patriarchy justifies giving males the position of authority. As a consequence, female labour is inflexible: women cannot make rational choices about how to invest their time, energy and other resources. In the traditional gender division of labour, women do more of every type of work in their communities compared to men. For instance their contribution is greater at the household level with regard to reproductive and productive roles. It is also heavier in the wider community. Women take responsibility for crop farming, harvesting and post harvesting activities. At the community level they are engaged in such community activities such as maintaining springs and wells. The culturally based allocation of roles and activities overloads women, interferes with the efficient production of food (Munene & Schwartz, 1999) and threatens food security in the home.

The economy of affection: A cultural interface that blocks growth

An analysis of traditional social structures in Africa suggests additional links to cultural values. Within the traditionally organised, stable social systems that characterised village life, African values formed a coherent whole that allowed Africans to organise themselves productively. Productive indigenous organisations included collective house building, cultivation, irrigation, and harvesting (Iguisi, 1995). Hyden labelled the traditional practice of mutual help, when it is practised in the context of a market economy, the economy of affection. He defined it as 'a network of support, communications, and interaction among structurally defined groups connected by blood, kin, community, and other affinities' (Hyden, 1983, p.8).

Although such values of mutual help and solidarity worked well for indigenous organisations, they appear to wreak havoc with the operation of capitalist-oriented bureaucracies in Africa. The economy of affection imposes particular social obligations on public office holders, perpetuates localism, and undermines the emergence of a cosmopolitan outlook. It is manifest in tribalism, nepotism, and sectarianism. Illfe (1983) described the same phenomenon (of mutual help gone wrong) as libertine pragmatism: an economy, which encourages acquisition for the limited purpose of servicing the needs of perceived dependants, including friends. Because all available wealth is devoted to meeting the immediate needs of dependants, accumulation of the savings and property needed to develop productivity over time does not occur. The resilience of the traditional institutions of the economy of affection in the face of attempts at socio-economic change in Africa prevents the emergence and penetration of productive capitalist structures. We next discuss an early study that illuminates this process.

Nasfsiger (1969) examined the effects of extended family systems on the performance of small firms in Algeria. Extended family systems are systems 'of shared rights and obligations encompassing a large number of near and distant relatives'. Among the assumptions of such systems are: consumption, development, and failure are collective; the collective selects which individuals should be pushed forward to devote themselves to achievement; all share in an individual member's success; successful individuals are obligated to the others, though they do not have to meet obligations immediately; the family is a key source of contacts.

Nasfsiger found that extended family systems were associated with more apprenticeship training and greater creation of new organisations. They related negatively, however, to the expansion of organisations. These findings can be explained by the operation of the economy of affection. The values of mutual self-help directly encourage and support apprenticeship training and the creation of new organisations or businesses. On the other hand, growth of business is difficult or impossible under a system that obliges individual entrepreneurs to transfer any excess resources to their family rather than investing them in growth of their business.

Causality in sub-Saharan Africa: An anti-scientific cultural interface

Yet another cultural interface that is problematic for development in sub-Saharan Africa revolves around the understanding of causality. Both in contacts with non-Africans and among Africans, the prevailing conceptions of causality often clash with solving problems and formulating plans in a scientific, empirically based manner. Gyekye (1997) claims that African cultures are ultimately guided by religion (see also Mbiti, 1969 and Parrinder, 1962) and by the faculty of conviction rather than by the faculty of reason. In support of this thesis, he notes that sub-Saharan Africans typically turn to the supernatural world and reject empirical causation whenever a misfortune befalls them. This, he argues, weakens the scientific basis for understanding and mastering the environment in Africa and marginalises sustained scientific and intellectual quest. The problem is so deeply rooted that even empirically oriented proverbs are used to end disputes, when brought into discussions in village councils, rather than to create a basis for further inquiry (Gyekye, 1997). As a result of this cultural orientation, Africans are likely to draw upon rules and dictates of superiors to resolve difficult negotiations, rather than to examine all sides of an issue without preconceptions in order to find innovative and creative solutions.

This non-scientific understanding of causality is one expression of the low importance attributed to the cultural orientation of intellectual autonomy and the high importance attributed to embeddedness in Africa. A major consequence of this cultural orientation is the continued existence of a non-science-based technology in (black) Africa. Science-based technology took root in much of the world in the nineteenth century. It relies on systematic testing and evaluation of tools and products, their constant refinement and improvement, and their widespread distribution to the public. Gyekye (1997) contrasted this with African healing practices. These have always remained the privilege of a selected few, maintained as esoteric knowledge unavailable for scientific testing and refinement. Only with the recent European interest in African herbal medicine has a broader spectrum of Africans begun to have access to the hoarded knowledge and skills of traditional African healers. The implements and techniques that Africans developed for their own use may have been efficient within their specific environment, but their weak scientific base hindered and stunted the growth of better technologies (Gyekye, 1997).

Social capital: A cultural interface that can promote development

The concept of social capital has become increasingly central in development literature (Woolcock & Narayan, 2000), but the construct's popularity has been accompanied by numerous controversies.

The strength of social capital as a construct for understanding development lies in its interpersonal or inter-group character.[6] This is also the character that qualifies it to be treated as an interface. In this study we define social capital as the coming together of compatible institutions. Because of the importance we attach to social capital in the study of poverty and moving out of poverty, we will address some of the emerging controversies to clarify how we intend to use the construct.

Recent controversies surrounding social capital

Four controversies regarding social capital are relevant here. First there are questions about whether social capital resides at the individual or at the community level. Second there are doubts about whether social capital can be used for purely private gain or whether its outcomes are always shared by some other people. A third controversy questions the relevance of the construct itself, with some writers asserting that the concept of social capital is redundant because it adds nothing to the general concept of capital. A fourth controversy, stemming from the above, regards whether or not it is possible to create social capital in the short or medium term.

Regarding the first controversy we suggest that social capital resides at both the individual and the community levels (See Briggs, 1998). However it can be deployed only at the interpersonal or inter-group level. On the second controversy, we argue that it is contradictory to think of social capital as private capital. We could only do so if we reduce social capital to an intrapersonal drive, something it obviously is not. Social capital can remain latent but, when deployed, it must profit at least one other person or group in addition to the individual. If social capital is used exploitatively, such as in a situation where trust is betrayed, then it ceases to be social capital, because by definition social capital is about mutual gain. An act of betrayal destroys social capital within the community. On the other hand, an act that honours trust serves to enhance existing social capital.

A related problem is whether it is possible to export social capital. To appreciate this controversy, imagine the following scenario that is only too real in Uganda and other African countries (see for instance Kasozi, 2003). A development manager in an NGO invests hundreds of thousands of dollars to implement a safe water project in a district. In one village the intervention is successful. New sources of water are provided and old ones are modernised. The villagers learn to value clean, safe water and the sources from which the water is drawn, and to maintain these sources. The value of safe and clean water becomes institutionalised in this village. In the next village the same intervention fails miserably. Even before the project ends, the new sources of safe water break down. The villagers collect water wherever they can, and do not try to repair the sources, looking to the NGO to do so instead.

Research conducted during and after the intervention shows that there was higher social capital in the village where the intervention was successful and less where the intervention failed (Kasozi, 2003; Iga, 2001). What should development practitioners recommend to their superiors to do to improve the situation in the second village? The answers depend on whether one believes that social capital can be exported. If it can be exported, the answer might be to undertake training of the villagers where the intervention failed to acquire the same kind of characteristics such as norms, attitudes, beliefs, motivations and values that we find in the more successful village and which are now considered as aspects of social capital. Our view that social capital cannot be exported suggests instead that a solution that is likely to succeed in the short run is to identify the institutions that were instrumental in 'demotivating' or preventing the villagers from taking up the offer/intervention and redesigning the project in such a way that these institutions are not threatened by the new social order being created by the project. We illustrate this point in detail in Chapter 5. Our recommendation is derived from our position that social capital is boundary specific and not exportable outside a community or a functioning network. That is, the interactional nature of social capital and its embeddedness in social relations prevent its exportation through imitation, modelling or training in the short and medium term.

The third controversy concerns the relevance of the construct social capital. One camp calls the term a misnomer that adds nothing to our stock of knowledge. These critics usually focus on the 'capital' aspect of the construct. They argue that social capital does not meet the parameters essential for qualifying as capital such as durability and distinctiveness (Arrow, 2000; Solow, 2000). Those who consider the construct to be useful focus on the social aspect of the construct (e.g. Ostrom, 2000 and Uphoff, 2000). They argue that it is measurable, that it enjoys operational distinctiveness, and that it complements other forms of capital (Narayan, 1997; Uphoff, 2000; Ostrom, 2000). We share this view.

The fourth controversy is whether or not it is possible to create social capital in the short or medium term. Is it possible and worthwhile to invest in the creation of social capital? To address this controversy, we must further clarify what we mean by social capital.

Drawing on the various usages in the literature (e.g., Adler & Kwon, 2002; Nahapiet & Goshal, 1998; Uphoff, 2000), we conceptualise social capital as the sharing by members of a community of a set of cognitions (beliefs, values, attitudes, expectations and knowledge) which they intentionally sustain through structures such as roles, rules, and networks. These shared cognitions motivate communities and their members to protect, maintain, and enhance their relationships. They enable people to reach similar judgements and evaluations of what outcomes are desirable and undesirable and what behaviour is rational or not. This promotes the assumption that 'others' are trustworthy and leads individuals to believe they can draw on 'others' for cooperative action when necessary. Because these shared cognitions can motivate community members to cooperate in joint pursuits, they are the backbone of community development (Vygotsky, 1978).

In the following two chapters we discuss values and knowledge respectively because they are the most researched aspects of the cognitive component of social capital. Chapter 4 discusses one of the value theories used to pass judgement and to set standards by which societies determine their way of life. Chapter 5 discusses the work of Vygotsky who shows how knowledge necessary for a community to develop is created and retained through community action.

People experience social capital more concretely at the level of structures (Uphoff, 2000). The purpose of structures is to institutionalise an idea that is valued by making it more concrete through repeated activities and actions. As a component of social capital, structures are concrete only at the level of being objective rather than being physical. The more researched structures include networks, to be discussed in Chapter 5. Others are rules, roles, procedures, and norms.

Figure 3.1 illustrates the feedback loops among constructs that constitute and define social capital as used by us. Structured encounters, characterised by compatible or

Figure 3.1: Conceptual definition of social capital

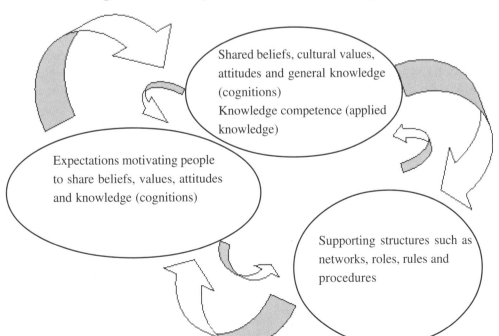

Shared beliefs, cultural values, attitudes and general knowledge (cognitions)
Knowledge competence (applied knowledge)

Expectations motivating people to share beliefs, values, attitudes and knowledge (cognitions)

Supporting structures such as networks, roles, rules and procedures shared norms, rules, and membership in networks, provide experiences that generate normative expectations that individuals hold for one another (Turner, 2000). These expectations, in turn, serve to motivate and sustain shared cognitions (beliefs, values, etc.) and reinforce the compatible structures that individuals and communities share. For instance, the expectations that are grounded in the cultural values of hierarchy, embeddedness and patriarchy have contributed to the establishment and maintenance of a monolithic political system in Uganda for over 33 years, either as a formal single party system or as a Movement system of government. Conversely, in West European communities that share values of autonomy and egalitarianism, the emergent expectations have supported social structures that institutionalise multiparty democracy. Thus compatible social structures and institutionalised behaviour, socially generated expectations, and cognitions reciprocally influence and support one another.

A study of managers from African and West European countries demonstrates this phenomenon (Munene, Schwartz, & Smith, 2000). Managers in African nations, which are high on hierarchy and embeddedness compared to donor nations, turned to their bosses and rules for guidance. Managers in donor nations, high in egalitarianism and intellectual autonomy, turned to colleagues and subordinates and to their 'own experience'. The behaviour of the African managers was compatible with the shared value expectations in their culture, and the very different behaviour of the West European managers was compatible with the opposing shared value expectations in their culture. This and other examples to be cited later indicate that social capital may be understood as a congruent combination of shared cognitions, institutionalised overt behaviour and expectations that motivate and lead to further sharing of cognitions.

By changing the shared cognitions of a group of people –generating new shared beliefs, values or attitudes, it is possible to create opportunities for altering institutionalised behaviour and expectations, roles and rules. The next chapter demonstrates how shared values, one aspect of social capital, can be measured and used to explain aspects of behaviours related to poverty alleviation. Chapters 5 and 7 provide case studies of shared beliefs and attitudes that changed through deliberate manipulations. It is nearly impossible, however, to change the other components of social capital without changing shared cognitions first. A good example of the difficulties involved in manipulating the structural components of social capital before changing cognitions is the attempt to reform the Uganda public service in our discussions of the cultural interfaces above.[7] Chapters 5 and 7 describe how a community and individuals resisted change and how this resistance was overcome. They show that much of the resistance to change was due to lack of knowledge, and to beliefs, values and attitudes that were incompatible with the solutions available to the villagers described in those chapters.

Bonding and bridging: The mechanisms of social capital and their value foundations

Putnam et al. (1993) identify two mechanisms of social capital, namely bonding and bridging. Bridging refers to the activity of connecting an identifiable actor such as networks, communities and individuals to other actors. Through bridging activities, groups and communities obtain skills, information, and other resources they need to overcome their own shortages of resources, shortages that prevent them from developing and progressing in the directions they desire (Temkin & Rohe, 1998). Bridging can link networks in the same community. It is even more critical, however, for linking networks that are more distant and therefore have little contact (Granovetter, 1973). Bonding refers to the commitments individuals or groups make to one another, commitments that lead to voluntarily helping acquaintances or the community. Bonding is grounded in trust and reciprocity. Two recent refinements of the indicators of bonding may further clarify what it is. The first refers to bonding as an overall sense of attachment and loyalty among neighbourhood residents or the commitment of residents to each other and to their environs (Temkin & Rohe, 1998). The second sees bonding as expressed in the social support people give and receive to help solve daily problems of survival (Briggs, 1998). Both the bonding and bridging mechanisms of social capital are crucial in promoting community development (see Chapters 5 and 7). That is, in order to develop, a community needs members who are willing, committed and able to invest in one another and in the larger group (bonding). And, because no community or individual lives in isolation, it needs members who act to link it to other communities and to the wider society in order to tap new resources required to progress (bridging).

Cultural value orientations that underlie social capital

Different cultural value orientations underlie and rationalise the two mechanisms of social capital. Cultural embeddedness can serve as the grounding for bonding expressed in close attachment to other members of one's community. In societies whose culture emphasises embeddedness values (e.g., forgiving, security, social order, reciprocation of favours), solidarity with others in the community, trust and tolerance of in-group members are normal states of affairs. It is crucial for people to get along smoothly and to maintain stable relationships within their group. Those who violate these taken-for-granted expectations pose a serious threat and are likely to be ostracised. Putnam (1993) described just such a cultural ambience as playing a key role in laying the foundation for good governance and economic development in northern Italy. This was the prevailing cultural ambience in much of sub-Saharan Africa during the last century, and recent research indicates that it prevails today (Schwartz, 2004).

When societies become more complex and extended kinship ties lose their central role in bonding societal members together, cultural embeddedness can no longer provide grounds for the bonding mechanisms that generate social capital. Individuals no longer identify strongly with many other community members, so feelings of closeness and identification are no longer adequate to motivate voluntary helpful acts. Individuals become more autonomous actors who pursue their own interests. Cultivation of one's own unique ideas, talents, preferences and feelings does not produce a commitment to the welfare of others. Unless another basis for social solidarity is found, bonding breaks down.

As societies develop economically and autonomy spreads, an alternative way for resolving the interdependency among individuals and groups must be found. One solution that has emerged is to socialise societal members to internalise commitments to egalitarian values (equality, social justice, freedom, responsibility, and honesty). The need for such commitments is not obvious to autonomous individuals, but without them, societies cannot run smoothly. Hence, social institutions emerge that inculcate these commitments through formal and informal socialisation that conveys and reinforces the understanding that others'welfare is important and should be promoted (Schwartz, 1999, 2004).

The egalitarian cultural value orientation of such societies propagates a view of individuals as moral equals who share basic interests. People are exhorted to behave responsibly towards one another, helping and co-operating voluntarily, out of an internalised belief in the desirability of promoting everyone's welfare. West European cultures are high in egalitarianism, whereas sub-Saharan African cultures are low on egalitarianism but high on embeddedness, as noted in the research mentioned above (Munene et al,2000; Schwartz, 2003). Bonding can be based on rational, voluntary concern for others in societies characterised by an egalitarian culture. Egalitarianism provides a motivational basis for supportive relations among people even when the individual is viewed as autonomous.

The bridging mechanism of social capital is grounded in another type of cultural value orientation. Bridging becomes critical when a community or an individual runs out of material or informational resources to cope with or solve problems. At this stage, learning and eventually development can take place only if a helping hand is obtained from outside. Bridging through social connections can link the community or individual to others who can give a helping hand and provide leverage in solving the problems (Temkin and Rohe, 1998). Bridging activities depend on individual actors who undertake them (Briggs, 1998; Granovetter, 1973). These actors must be motivated to find ways to surmount problems, to take actions that will enable greater control over the environment. The cultural value orientation of Mastery (Schwartz, 1999) can serve as the grounding for the motivation to serve as a bridge.

As we saw earlier, Mastery concerns the degree to which groups and individuals seek to master, change and control the material and social environment. In high mastery cultures, there is an emphasis on assertively controlling and exploiting the environment as a means to survive and progress. Values that are emphasised include being successful, capable, ambitious, daring, independent, and choosing one's own goals. In societies high on mastery, individuals and groups are encouraged to actively seek knowledge, information, and ties that will enable them to solve problems. Hence a mastery culture promotes the use of bridging to promote social capital. Compared with other regions of the world, sub-Saharan Africa is relatively high on the cultural orientation of mastery. So there are cultural grounds in Africa for this mechanism of generating social capital. On the other hand, sub-Saharan Africa is relatively low on the other cultural orientation especially likely to promote bridging-intellectual autonomy. This cultural value orientation encourages and gives legitimacy to individuals' pursuit of their own ideas, and unique talents and skills. It thereby helps to generate new ways of coping with problems both through individual ingenuity and seeking new knowledge and solutions from outside traditional networks. Figure 3.2 presents the relationship between the two mechanisms of social capital and the cultural value orientations that might promote them.

Figure 3.2 indicates the role social capital plays in development. It also proposes that bonding and bridging mechanisms are both grounded in cultural values. This study draws upon the seven cultural value orientations in the Schwartz (1999, 2004) model.

Figure 3.2: Culture, social capital and development

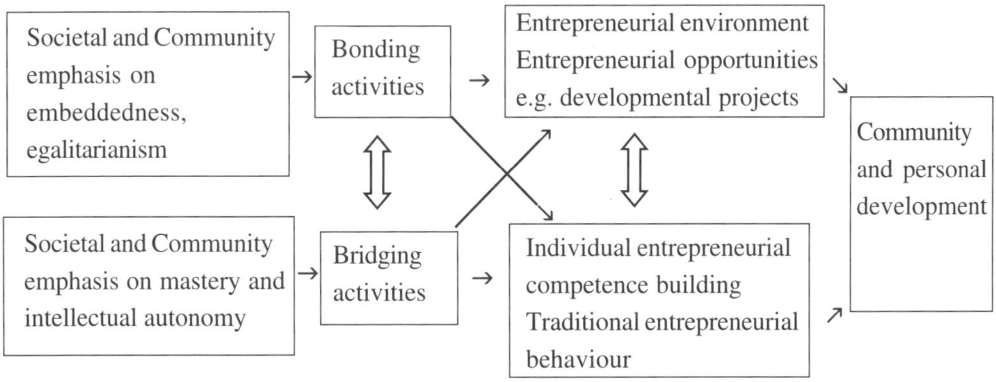

Other cultural values may also underlie and affect the development of social capital. The figure also indicates that bonding and bridging must come together in order to create the environment necessary for projects to be set up well and for individuals to take advantage of these projects. When we have this kind of combination we have the cultural interface needed for development.

Conclusion

This chapter emphasises the central role that culture plays in development. Our effort throughout has been to demonstrate that the encompassing culture influences the everyday experiences of people in a community or society. The availability of data to characterise the broad culture of five sub-Saharan African countries and of the major European donor countries enabled us to specify the cultural orientations likely to influence everyday life in Africa and to influence interaction between Africans and Europeans. The model of cultural value orientations allowed us to focus on the impact of culture both on the individuals and on the collectivities in which they are embedded.

In this chapter we have argued that an understanding of the influence of culture (culture as action) on everyday behaviour is only a first step in using culture to analyse development in Africa. The second and a more crucial step is to recognise the impact of contact between cultures when development projects bring Africans into contact with individuals or ideas from other societies. Africans have endured a recent intensive experience of colonisation and are probably continuing to face a neo-colonising experience today. We have focused on the impact of culture contact by introducing the concept of cultural interface. We illustrated the cultural interface by examining the failure of a $500,000 project in the Ugandan Reform Programme. The innovators proposed new criteria for establishing pay in the public service that were based on cultural assumptions imported from societies characterised by cultural emphases on autonomy and egalitarianism. A clash was inevitable because the civil servants to whom these criteria were to apply take for granted an opposing set of cultural emphases that characterise Ugandan culture – hierarchy and embeddedness. We illustrated another problematic cultural interface, one encountered in African work settings set up according to bureaucratic models. This is the clash between cultural obligations to give primacy above all to mutual help among close kin or friends (the economy of affection) versus the cultural expectations that govern the commitment to one's job in the bureaucracy and to preserving the interests of the organisation. Both of these examples illustrate conflict-ridden cultural interfaces. We identified the source of conflict as the coming together of incompatible cultural institutions such as egalitarian and hierarchical value orientations in the Uganda Reform Programme example.

Drawing on existing analyses of social capital, we described social capital as the presence of compatible and complementary institutions in a community that generate a harmonious cultural interface. We adopted a conceptual definition of social capital that views it as consisting of three reciprocally interdependent components. These are shared cognitions such as beliefs, attitudes, values, and knowledge; institutional structures in which social actors interact harmoniously such as networks, norms and rules; and shared expectations and motivations for behaviour and cognitions that emerge through individual and communal experiences of interaction within the structures. We discussed the bonding and bridging mechanisms that help in generating social capital and the cultural value orientations that underlie these mechanisms. The following two chapters build on the ideas discussed here. Chapter 4 focuses on cultural value orientations and individual values and how these may influence behaviour in development projects. Chapter 5 addresses knowledge and skills (competences) as well as networks and their roles in community and individual well-being.

---

1. Marris (1968) describes how extended families in North Africa are parasites on the entrepreneur, thereby preventing entrepreneurship. Many Africans who have set up their own businesses will find this familiar. Achebe describes the tragic consequence of rapid change familiar to Africans, a West African bureaucrat who indirectly causes the death of two of his people.

2. This dimension was previously called 'Conservatism vs. Autonomy (Schwartz, 1994a, 1996, Schwartz & Ross, 1995; Smith & Schwartz, 1997). Schwartz changed the label in order to emphasise the central notion of the person as part of the collectivity and to avoid misunderstandings that have arisen in the ujse of the earlier label. Relations of this dimension and those to follow with the well known cultural dimensions proposed by Hofstede (1980) and Markus & Kitayama (1991) are discussed in Schwartz (2004), in Schwartz & Ross (1995) and Sagiv & Schwartz (2000).

3. An interesting variant form of cultural interface may occur in the life of the individual actor. S/he may be called upon to behave simultaneously, or in close temporal proximity, according to the rules or expectations of culturally different institutions. For instance s/he may be torn between the incompatible rules of economic and religious institutions.

4. See also Nasfsiger (1969) who examined the effects of the extended family system on the performance of small firms in Nigeria.

5. In the Ugandan Public Service, permanent secretary is the highest administrive post in a

ministry. Until recently, qualifying for this post required no less than 15 years in the Service, during which the candidate was expected to serve in virtually all posts in the Service. Second in the hierarchy is the post of director, a technical position held by a person with appropriate technical qualifications. A director, say of Health, is in charge of several departments in the Ministry of Health and is trained in medicine or related fields. The third executive post is the commissioner, also a technical post. A commission heads a department under a directorate. Commissioners in large ministries often have more work than permanent secretaries in less demanding ministries.

6. We follow Putnam's (1993) conceptualisation of social capital, rather than Coleman's (1988).

7. We refer especially to 'Culture-Task Interface: The Consequences of the Equity Principle in an Institutional Reform Programme'.

4
Values and Economic Success in Uganda: An Empirical Study

In this chapter we present empirical findings using a recent theory of values with data from over 60,000 respondents in 65 countries from all inhabited continents. First, we discuss cultural values in Uganda compared with other countries in greater detail than has been done so far, using the Schwartz (1999, 2003) model of cultural value orientations. Second, we examine cultural values in the Ugandan districts and regions we studied, each with its particular ethnic composition. Third, we consider individual rather than cultural values and examine relations of individual differences in values to participation in development projects and to economic performance and success.

Comparing Uganda to other nations

We compare the cultural profile of Uganda with that of other countries on the seven cultural value orientations on which national cultures are discriminated: embeddedness, intellectual and affective autonomy, hierarchy, egalitarianism, mastery and harmony.

We first examined descriptions of culture in sub-Saharan Africa found in research by historians, anthropologists and other scholars who have written about the continent. This is in keeping with Nsamenang and Dawes (1998) who suggest that African psychologists should commence their psychological enquiries by examining historical and anthropological experiences to avoid seeing psychological universals where they do not exist. This may easily happen when they uncritically apply existing psychological theories to African data. The writings of several African scholars (e.g., Akong'a, 1995; Ahiazu, 1995; Mbiti, 1969, and Gyekye, 1995, 1997) suggest that there is a shared African cultural system that is relevant to economic performance. From this literature, we derived a set of hypotheses regarding the cultural value profile that might characterise Black African nations in general and Uganda in particular and that might distinguish them from other nations.

Onwuejeogwu (1995) provided a list of the ideals or values that motivate African peoples and by which they evaluate their activities. Love of life and family are seen as ends in themselves and as the foundations of human society. Africans maintain a sense of solidarity with the collectivity from the past to the present and into the future by emphasising enduring, close ties to family throughout the generations. The kinship and extended family systems, age-grade institutions, and relations of respect for authority and old age express the importance of these values and give them institutional support. This mode of valuing parallels Embeddedness and Hierarchy cultural values.

Onwuejeogwu (1995, paraphrased) describes Africans as guided in their daily lives by numerous specific values or beliefs that maintain their general values:

1. The world is an integrated whole in which all occurrences are traceable to one source.

2. Proverbs should ground practical/common sense thinking.
3. Theoretical thinking should be rooted in mysticism.
4. Truth is context-specific (depending on one's relationship with or the status of its source).
5. Trust relatives but not strangers.
6. Maintain order in life by avoiding unnecessary risks.
7. Wisdom is thought and behaviour in harmony with one's ancestors.
8. Wisdom is making the best of available opportunities.
9. Success or failure depend on help or hindrance of powerful others (e.g. godparents).
10. Advancement depends on allegiance to powerful groups or individuals.

These ten African value orientations relate clearly to the cultural values defined by Schwartz. Orientations 2, 3, 4,5,6,9, and 10 are views expressive of a culture that emphasises Embeddedness values, because they focus on the person as part of a larger collectivity that is the source of meaning in their lives and that links them to tradition. These same orientations (minus 6 but including 7) are also specific expressions of Hierarchy values. They share an emphasis on a traditional, status-differentiated organisation of social groups. Orientations 1 and 6 are expressions of Embeddedness and Harmony values.

In contrast, many of these orientations oppose the emphases of Autonomy (2, 3, 4, 7,9,10 oppose Intellectual Autonomy; 6 opposes Affective Autonomy). They conflict with the assumption of Autonomy that individuals derive meaning from their unique ideas, actions, and outlooks. Orientations 4, 5, 9 and 10 also oppose Egalitarianism, which rejects status differentiation and emphasises the moral equality of individuals. The relation of Mastery values to these presumed African orientations is less clear cut. On the one hand, 8 is compatible with Mastery values that justify exploiting the social and natural environment; but 6 and 9 conflict with Mastery values because they call for cautiousness and reliance on others rather than initiative and assertiveness.

Analyses of traditional social structures in Africa suggest additional links to cultural value orientations. Within the traditionally organised, stable social systems that characterised village life, African values presumably formed a coherent whole that allowed the people to organise themselves productively (Hyden, 1983; Iguisi, 1995). Indigenous organisations included collective house building, cultivation, irrigation, and harvesting (Iguisi, 1995). Hyden (1983) as discussed in the last chapter, described, "a network of support, communications, and interaction among structurally defined groups connected by blood, kin, community, and other affinities" (p.8). These preferred relationships in Africa also express Embeddedness and Hierarchy.

As we saw earlier, according to some analysts, when these modes of work relations are maintained in the context of a market economy, they seriously interfere with productivity and work against modern bureaucratic methods. These authors evidently find that Autonomy and Egalitarianism value orientations, more suitable to Western bureaucracies, are lacking in Africa. Whether changing modes of organisation to fit prevailing values or changing values to fit modes of organisation will better foster development is both a value judgement and a practical question. However, one conclusion is clear. Analysts of Black African societies point to a shared cultural value system that supposedly crosses national boundaries. This system is characterised by an emphasis on Embeddedness and Hierarchy at the expense of Autonomy and Egalitarianism. These analysts imply no distinctive Black African profile on the Mastery-Harmony cultural dimension.

One might object that anthropological studies of African culture have pointed to the uniqueness of cultures across this vast continent rather than to their similarities. However, the argument for cultural relatedness across Africa has been cogently made by a number of African philosophers (see Chapter 3). Most critical has been the shared struggle to modernise and develop in order to meet basic survival needs. This suggests that sub-Saharan African culture will now emphasise Mastery at the expense of Harmony.

Two other elements of shared African culture are relevant to our hypotheses. As we saw in Chapter 3, African cultures are ultimately guided by religion rather than reason (Mbiti, 1969; Parrinder, 1962, Gyekye, 1995, 1997). As a result, little value is placed on sustained scientific or intellectual quest (i.e., low Intellectual Autonomy). A related feature of the culture has been the absence of a science-based technology that might foster the improvement of products and techniques through public scrutiny and evaluation (Gyekye, 1997). Instead, knowledge has been closely guarded by elites (e.g. healers), stunting the growth of adaptive technologies. This implies strong emphasis on Hierarchy rather than Intellectual Autonomy and Egalitarianism.

Are these characterisations of a broad African culture supported by empirical analyses of values? We address this question with data obtained in the current study and in earlier work by Schwartz. Schwartz (1994a, 1999) gathered values data from over 60,000 respondents in 65 different nations around the world. Two sets of matched samples were studied: school teachers mostly from urban areas (54 nations), and university or college students (54 nations; 14 non-overlapping nations), all from the dominant cultural groups. Samples average about 200 respondents. Teachers are the focal occupational group. They play a key role in value socialisation. Moreover, their educational level and status relative to others is similar across nations, thereby roughly providing a control for major potential confounding variables. Students were included in order to check the robustness of findings by assessing the extent to which national differences replicate in an independent set of matched samples. Data from Black African samples were obtained in Ghana, Nigeria, South Africa and Zimbabwe, in addition to Uganda.

Values were measured with the Schwartz Value Survey (SVS) (Schwartz, 1992), including 56 or 57 single values, each followed by a brief parenthetical explanation. Respondents indicated the importance of each value as a guiding principle in their own lives, using a 9-point scale. The survey was administered anonymously in the respondents' native language or in the prevailing common language in the country (i.e. English in Uganda and Anglophone Africa). Exemplary values used to form each cultural value orientation were given earlier (see Chapter 3), when the cultural value orientations were defined. We used only those 44 values that had demonstrated cross-cultural equivalence of meaning based on within-culture analyses in earlier studies.

Table 4.1. Mean importance ratings and ranks of cultural values (SVS) in selected African and European countries based on teacher samples from 54 nations

Nations	Harmony	Embedded-ness	Hierarchy	Mastery	Affective Autonomy	Intellectual Autonomy	Egalitarianism
Denmark (n=852)	4.32	3.29	1.90	3.92	4.01	4.77	5.14
	(21)	(51)	(53)	(36)	(5)	(9.5)	(7)
Netherlands (n=306)	4.19	3.36	2.09	4.00	3.64	4.77	5.09
	(30)	(50)	(39)	(40)	(10)	(9.5)	(9)
West Germany (n=335)	4.69	3.12	2.04	3.94	3.76	4.92	5.13
	(10)	(53)	(42)	(37)	(9)	(3)	(8)
Ghana (n=209)	3.44	4.30	2.68	4.34	2.16	3.94	4.85
	(52)	(3)	(18)	(2.5)	(54)	(45)	(39)
Zimbabwe (n=331)	3.55	4.06	2.85	4.34	3.56	3.90	4.29
	(47)	(25)	(10)	(2.5)	(25)	(47)	(50)
Uganda (n=428)	3.96	4.14	3.60	4.17	3.00	3.84	4.20
	(45)	(16)	(3)	(13)	(40)	(51)	(52)

Note: 1 = Highest possible rank; 54 = Lowest possible rank.

For each sample, the average importance rating given to the single values that comprise each value orientation was computed. The seven averages constituted the scores of cultural values for the sample. In the case of nations in which multiple samples were available, scores of all samples were averaged to yield the national profile.

Based on the analyses of African societies reported on the previous page, we hypothesised that there is a shared Black African cultural value profile that will characterise Uganda as well. We expected samples from these nations to attribute high importance to Embeddedness and Hierarchy and low importance to Autonomy (both Affective and Intellectual) and Egalitarianism. The literature suggested, though less clearly, that Mastery would be more important than Harmony.

The ratings of the importance attributed by each sample to each of the seven cultural value orientations are shown in Table 4.1 for the teacher samples. We compare these to the cultural value profiles of three West European nations that have been active as donors in Uganda. In parentheses following the importance ratings, we list the ranks of each nation as compared to the full set of samples from 54 nations. Ranks are from 1 (the national sample that rated the value most important), to 54 (the national sample that rated it least important). The European samples are grouped in the upper part of the Table and the four Black African samples are grouped in the lower part the Table.

Table 4.1 shows no overlap between the importance attributed to each of the seven cultural values in the three West European nations and in the three African nations. Embeddedness, Hierarchy, and Mastery were more important in every one of the African nations than in any of the West European nations. Egalitarianism, Intellectual Autonomy, Affective Autonomy and Harmony were more important in every one of the West European nations than in all of the African nations. Applying Mann-Whitney U-tests to the ranks, the West European and African samples differ significantly, in the hypothesised directions, in their emphases on all seven cultural values (all $p<0.01$, except for Affective Autonomy, $p<0.02$).

The data reveal that these two groups of nations are characterised by different cultural value profiles. The data also show substantial homogeneity of cultural orientations among the three West European nations and among the African nations. The findings for the African nations provide strong support for the hypothesised pattern derived from the literature on African culture. The African nations were especially high on Hierarchy, Mastery and Embeddedness and low on Egalitarianism, Intellectual Autonomy, and Harmony. The Ugandan cultural profile was consistent with the other Black African nations.

Table 4.2 presents parallel data that reflect the robustness of the findings from teachers. Here, student samples from five Black African nations are compared with student samples from three West European donor nations. Ranks are based on 54 different nations. For six cultural value orientations, there is no overlap whatsoever in ranks between the African and West European nations. Embeddedness and Hierarchy are more important in Africa than in Western Europe, and Egalitarianism, Affective Autonomy, Intellectual Autonomy, and Harmony are more important in Western Europe than in Africa (all $p<0.01$ by Mann-Whitney U-test). These findings replicate the pattern based on teacher samples.

There is no difference between European and African student samples on Mastery values. The high importance of Mastery at the expense of Harmony was implied by

Table 4.2 Mean importance ratings and ranks of cultural values (SVS) in selected African and European countries based on student samples from 54 nations

Nations	Harmony	Embedded-ness	Hierarchy	Mastery	Affective Autonomy	Intellectual Autonomy	Egalitarianism
England (n=158)	4.01 (22)	3.14 (48)	2.47 (28)	4.33 (18.5)	4.65 (1)	4.80 (16)	4.82 (16)
Netherlands (n=495)	3.90 (34)	3.02 (51)	1.99 (42)	4.37 (17)	4.61 (2)	4.92 (13)	4.97 (11)
West Germany (n=857)	4.68 (3)	2.83 (53)	1.89 (51)	4.13 (40)	4.49 (6)	5.14 (3)	5.05 (3)
Ghana (n=210)	3.62 (44)	4.24 (3)	2.79 (12)	4.21 (27)	2.82 (52)	3.83 (45)	4.60 (36)
Nigeria (n=111)	3.57 (50)	4.35 (2)	2.74 (13)	4.25 (22)	2.72 (54)	3.69 (53)	4.69 (28)
South Africa (n=128) (Black)	3.71 (40)	4.12 (5)	2.54 (24)	4.11 (41)	3.57 (39)	3.90 (47)	4.57 (37)
Zimbabwe (n=375)	3.61 (45)	4.05 (10)	2.57 (21)	4.45 (7)	3.44 (33)	3.73 (52)	4.30 (48.5)
Uganda (n=188)	3.83 (38)	4.15 (4)	3.06 (4)	4.33 (18.5)	2.81 (53)	3.81 (51)	4.30 (48.5)

Note: 1 = Highest possible rank; 54 = Lowest possible rank.

some but not all of the literature on Africa. Its occurrence in the teacher samples is consistent with Schwartz's (1993) proposal that low socio-economic levels are conducive to valuing and legitimising assertive exploitation of the natural and social environment, placing efforts to raise a low standard of living ahead of efforts to preserve nature and harmony. Among the student samples, however, there was no consistent cultural pattern. It should be noted that the Ugandan students, like the students from Zimbabwe and the African teachers, exhibited a substantial cultural emphasis on Mastery.

These findings increase our confidence in the conclusions from the teachers' data and provide further strong empirical support for African scholars' observations of their own culture. The empirical results provide little support for a view of African culture as encouraging Autonomy, like that propounded by Gyekye (1997). There may well be sources in African culture that encourage Autonomy, but the prevailing temper, at least in comparison to Western Europe, is an emphasis on Embeddedness and Hierarchy at the expense of Autonomy and Egalitarianism.

There is, of course, some variation in value importance both among the West European nations and among the African nations. Overall, however, this variation is small compared to the much larger variation between these sets of nations. This justifies viewing the African nations and the West European nations as broad cultural regions, at least in terms of their profiles on the seven cultural value orientations studied here.

The observed contrast between West European and African value profiles raises the problem of intercultural communication and creates a cultural interface plagued by opportunities for conflict (see Table 3.1 Chapter 2). It suggests that substantial misunderstanding, miscommunication, and mismatching of goals and interpretations of events will occur in contacts between people socialised in the West European donor nations and in the African client nations. The data suggest certain types of mismatch are especially likely. The basic conceptions of the nature of individuals and their relations to the group that prevail in the two sets of nations differ substantially. Africans are likely to emphasise the role of the individual as a group member who derives meaning from shared ideas, ideals, practices, and fate (Embeddedness). In contrast, West Europeans are more likely to view the individual as someone who derives meaning from his or her distinctive experiences, ideas, ideals, personality, and aspirations (Autonomy).

Assumptions about how best to elicit socially responsible behaviour also differ. Africans are likely to expect such behaviour to be controlled through a hierarchy of defined roles and regulations, as determined by accepted traditions and ensured by obedience (Hierarchy). In contrast, West Europeans are more likely to expect individuals to take personal responsibility, voluntarily following internalised norms based on negotiated understandings (Egalitarianism). Finally, the findings suggest that Ugandans and those from Zimbabwe are more likely than West Europeans to legitimise active exploitation of the environment to meet their needs, even at the expense of the natural environment (Mastery versus Harmony).

Comparing regions and districts within Uganda

The instrument used to measure values with the teacher and student samples was not intended for less educated populations such as the beneficiaries of the rural development projects we studied in Uganda. Consequently, we developed a simpler method that was suitable to this population as well as to adolescents and to the elderly. This new instrument, called the Portrait Values Questionnaire (PVQ), presents brief descriptions of 29 different people. It was validated in a study of adolescent girls from Uganda (for a full explication, see Schwartz, Lehman, & Roccas, 1999 and Schwartz, et al., 2001).

Each portrait consists of two sentences that characterise the person's goals, aspirations, and wishes, all expressive of a single type of value. For example:

> Thinking up new ideas and being creative is important to him. He likes to do things in his own original way.

> She looks for adventures and likes to take risks. She wants to have an exciting life.

By emphasising what is important to the person–the goals and wishes he or she pursues, the portraits describe the person's values rather than his or her behaviour or traits. Respondents indicate 'How much like you is this person' by checking one of six boxes labelled: very much like me, like me, somewhat like me, a little like me, not like me, and not like me at all.

There are several notable differences between the SVS used earlier and the new PVQ methods for measuring individuals' value priorities. First, the SVS asks for ratings of the importance of values as guiding principles in one's life, while the PVQ obtains judgements of the similarity of another person to oneself. Judgements of similarity are more common and easier to perform. Second, the stimuli in the SVS are a set of abstract, context-free values, while the stimuli in the PVQ are people, portrayed in terms of their goals, aspirations and wishes. People find it easier to respond to more concrete and contextualised concepts. Third, the SVS uses a nine-point numerical response scale with both labelled and unlabelled scale points, while the PVQ asks respondents to check one of six labelled boxes. Thus, the PVQ demands less finely tuned discriminations and requires no conversion of subjective judgements to a numerical scale. Most generally, the SVS elicits direct, self-conscious reports of one's values, while the PVQ measures values only indirectly.

Like the SVS, the PVQ is intended to measure both the types of values that discriminate among individuals and the types of values on which cultures vary. To test the PVQ's validity for measuring cultural values would require data from parallel samples in at least 20 different cultures. Such data are not yet available. Hence, we can only use the a priori, hypothesised indexes of the cultural value orientations to compute cultural value profiles for the samples from the Ugandan regions that we studied. The data we present next must therefore be viewed as very tentative. Moreover, the cultural value scores based on the PVQ cannot be compared with those based on the SVS because it is likely that each scale has different base rates for each value. Cultural comparisons using PVQ based scores are meaningful only to establish the relative importance of each cultural emphasis across the samples compared.

We administered the PVQ to the participants and to non-participant (controls) in the projects in each of the regions and districts studied. Table 4.3 presents the mean importance score for each cultural orientation in each district and region, across all respondents. Districts differed significantly on four cultural value orientations: Affective Autonomy, Intellectual Autonomy, Mastery and Embeddedness.

Table 4.3: Mean cultural value scores (PVQ) of Ugandan villages by district

Region	District	Harmony	Embeddedness	Hierarchy	Mastery	Affective Autonomy	Intellectual Autonomy	Egalitarianism
Western	Bushenyi (n=36)	3.52	3.13	2.57	2.98	2.57	3.02	3.26
	Kabale	3.33	3.06	2.59	3.08	2.83	2.92	3.33
Northern	Arua (n=29)	3.40	3.23	2.33	2.95	2.79	2.92	3.12
	Nebbi (n=47)	3.11	3.16	2.76	2.95	2.92	2.85	3.25
Central	Mpigi (n=45)	3.48	3.19	2.86	3.31	1.73	2.41	3.66
	Mukono (n=94)	3.14	3.22	2.85	3.15	1.92	2.63	3.69
	Masaka (n=103)	3.34	3.35	2.72	3.22	1.42	2.88	3.54
$F_{(6,382)}$	F	1.54	5.4*	2.9	6.1*	8.6**	8.2**	2.1

**p<.01; *p<.05

As noted, the PVQ-based culture scores may be used only to compare samples on each cultural orientation, not to infer the relative importance of the different cultural orientations. What we can ask is: How do the cultural profiles of the districts differ? And which districts exhibit profiles more or less like the African culture identified earlier, using a more valid instrument to measure cultural value orientations? Because of the substantial similarity of districts within each region on most orientations, we compare the three regions rather than the separate districts.

As compared with the North and West, the districts from the Central region show the most African cultural profile. Relative to the other regions, the Central region is very low in its cultural emphases on both types of Autonomy, high in its emphasis on Mastery, and somewhat high in its emphasis on Hierarchy and Embeddedness. This may seem surprising because the Central region is the most developed and the most exposed to Western influences.[1] It suggests that westernisation of values has had little if any impact on the values of the people who joined the development projects we studied. The Northern and Western regions differ little from one another.

Despite these differences, it is interesting to note that there is substantial agreement across districts regarding the relative importance of the seven cultural orientations. Egalitarianism and Harmony ranked among the most important orientations in all districts, Embeddedness and Mastery were next, then Intellectual Autonomy, Hierarchy, and Affective Autonomy. Thus, even the weak measurement of cultural orientations with the PVQ provides some evidence for a shared Ugandan culture.

Individual differences, participation in projects, and economic performance

We turn next to an examination of how differences between individuals in their personal values relate to whether they participate in development projects and to whether they gain economically from such participation. The cultural values approach employed thus far is inappropriate for this purpose as the dimensions of values that discriminate among individuals differ from those that discriminate among societies. We therefore employ the theory of individual value systems developed by Schwartz (1992) that applies to individuals. Below is a brief overview of those aspects of the theory essential for understanding the current research (see Schwartz, 1992 and 1994 for a full explication).

Each individual value expresses a type of motivational goal. The theory derived ten motivationally distinct types of values, presumed to encompass the range of values recognised across cultures, from an analysis of the universal requirements of human existence. Table 4.4 provides definitions of each motivationally distinct value in terms of its central goal.

Table 4.4: Definitions of ten individual values in terms of their core goals

Self-Direction: Independent thought and action—choosing, creating, exploring

Stimulation: Excitement, novelty and challenge in life

Hedonism: Pleasure and sensuous gratification for oneself

Achievement: Personal success through demonstrating competence according to social standards

Power: Social status and prestige, control or dominance over people and resources

Security: Safety, harmony and stability of society, of relationships and of self

Conformity: Restraint of actions, inclinations and impulses likely to upset or harm others or violate social expectations or norms

Tradition: Respect, commitment and acceptance of the customs and ideas that traditional culture or religion provide

Benevolence: Preservation and enhancement of the welfare of people with whom one is in frequent personal contact

Universalism: Understanding, appreciation, tolerance and protection for the welfare of all people and for nature

Cross-cultural research in 65 countries, using the SVS, verified that people discriminate implicitly among these types of values when rating their importance (Schwartz, 1992, Schwartz & Bardi, 2001). It has also upheld their claimed comprehensiveness. Recent research in five countries, using the PVQ, has added multi-method support for the discrimination of these ten values. There is evidence, moreover, from studies in 19 countries that these individual values relate meaningfully to a wide variety of behaviours (e.g., consumer purchases, co-operation and competition, behavioural style of those being counselled, delinquent behaviour, environmental behaviour, inter-group social contact, occupational choice, religious observance, and voting).

The ten values are dynamically related to one another. This is because actions taken in the pursuit of each value have psychological, practical, and social consequences that may conflict or may be compatible with the pursuit of other values. For example, the pursuit of achievement values often conflicts with the pursuit of benevolence values: seeking personal success for oneself is likely to obstruct actions aimed at enhancing the welfare of others who need one's help. Similarly, the pursuit of tradition values conflicts with the pursuit of stimulation values: accepting cultural and religious customs and ideas handed down from the past is likely to inhibit seeking novelty, challenge, and excitement. On the other hand, benevolence and conformity values are compatible because they entail behaving in a manner approved by one's close group. In addition, the pursuit of security is compatible with the pursuit of power since both stress avoiding uncertainty by controlling relationships and resources.

Because of these dynamic interrelations, the ten values form two sets of opposing higher-order values, arrayed on two bipolar dimensions. The first dimension – openness to change versus conservation – opposes values that emphasise one's own independent thought and action and favour change (self-direction and stimulation) to values that emphasise submissive self-restriction, preservation of traditional practices and protection of stability (security, conformity and tradition). The second dimension – self-transcendence versus self-enhancement – opposes values that emphasise acceptance of others as equals and concern for their welfare (universalism and benevolence) to values that emphasise the pursuit of one's relative success and dominance over others (power and achievement). Hedonism includes elements of both openness to change and self-enhancement.

We computed scores on each of the ten values for each participant and control group member from the development projects studied. These scores were based on responses to the PVQ. We distinguished two types of tradition values because the structural analyses indicated that the self-abnegation and customs/religion components of tradition were distinct in these samples.

We first ask whether personal value priorities were associated with participation in a development project. Strongly endorsing particular values might induce people to be more receptive to joining, leaving, or rejecting the opportunity to participate in a project in their community. Table 4.5 presents the mean value ratings of participants and non-participants in development projects. This comparison does not take into account the different sorts of projects in which people participated.

Participants differed from non-participants in development projects only with regard to the importance they attributed to two types of individual values, hedonism and security. Both these values were less important to participants than to non-participants. Thus, those who emphasise immediate pleasure and gratification (hedonism) were less likely to join or to maintain membership in development projects. We interpret this as linked to the fact that participation in development projects demands serious investment of energy, time and resources, with the rewards coming only over time. People who emphasise hedonism values are likely to find such demands unattractive and to be frustrated by the absence of immediate, pleasurable rewards.

The findings for security suggest that participation in projects may be unattractive for another reason. Projects demand change in the daily life of participants, adopting

Table 4.5. Mean personal value ratings of project participants and non-participants

Value	Participants (n=293)	Non-participant controls (n=105)
Power	2.74	2.67
Achievement	3.13	3.09
Hedonism	1.95*	2.49
Stimulation	2.08	2.14
Self-direction	2.95	2.98
Universalism	3.27	3.19
Benevolence	3.57	3.45
Conformity	3.28	3.16
Security	3.58*	3.79
Tradition: self-abnegation	2.59	2.60
Tradition: customs, religion	2.93	2.89

*Difference between groups is significant, p< 0.01.

new methods of work, learning new skills, taking risks on new activities that may upset current patterns of relationships in the family, activities that provide no assurance against failure. For those who emphasise security values, it is important to maintain the status quo, to preserve the secure environment and relationships they have developed, to avoid change and risk in order to avoid anxiety-arousing threats. They may therefore be hesitant to join projects until these are already widely accepted in the community and proven to be successful.

Next, we consider relations between personal value priorities and the motives participants reported for joining development projects. For example, we might expect those who emphasise openness to change values to join an innovative project more readily than those who emphasise conservation values. We might also expect those who emphasise self-enhancement values to be especially eager to join a project that promises economic advancement, while those who emphasise self-transcendence values might be more receptive to joining a project aimed at helping other members of the community.

Through factor analysis (see Chapter 6 for details of this analysis), we identified three distinct reasons for joining projects: to gain skills and knowledge, to help others, and to improve one's own and one's family's standard of living. We correlated personal value priorities with each of these motives (Table 4.6).

TheTable shows a number of interesting correlations. Note first that hedonism correlates negatively with all the three motives. Stimulation shows a similar pattern, though its relationship with helping non-kin others is not statistically reliable. This reinforces the conclusion regarding the effects of hedonism values on joining projects inferred from the data in Table 4.5. Valuing stimulation, excitement and novelty

Table 4.6: Correlations of basic individual values with motives for joining projects (n = 293)

Value	Type of motive		
	Gaining skills and knowledge	Helping non-kin others	Improving own and family's standard of living
Power	.36**	-.13*	-.03
Achievement	-.04	-.03	-.03
Hedonism	-.33**	-.16*	-.25**
Stimulation	-.27**	-.11	-.27**
Self-direction	.07	.00	.02
Universalism	.35**	.19**	.29**
Benevolence	-.08	.00	.05
Tradition	-.02	.04	.06
Conformity	.04	.07	.16*
Security	.17**	.20**	.17**

**p<0.01, *p<0.05

undermines all three of the prominent motivations to join projects. Individuals who emphasise hedonism and stimulation values are less interested than others in gaining skills and knowledge and in providing for the welfare of others through joining development projects.

The results for security values supplement our inferences about how these values affect the decision whether or not to participate in development projects. As noted, those who emphasise security values are less likely to join projects, probably out of fear of upsetting the status quo. Nonetheless, they may be motivated to join in order to gain the skills and knowledge that will enable them to master their environment – thereby enhancing their ability to avoid or control unanticipated threats. They are also motivated to join in order to aid others and improve standards of living – thereby creating a more secure environment for themselves and their families. Thus, if these rewards of participation in projects are salient in the situation and look promising, those who emphasise security values may overcome their reluctance to take risks and decide to join.

People who emphasise power values (gaining control over people and resources) are motivated to join projects for quite different reasons. In keeping with their basic values, these people look to the projects to enable them to gain the skills needed to master the environment – to pursue their own self-centred goals. Also in keeping with their self-enhancing orientation, they are not interested in projects for the sake of helping others. The other notable and consistent correlations are found for universalism values. Not surprisingly, people who emphasise these self-transcendence values are motivated to join projects to the extent that they perceive the projects as helping others

Table 4.7: Correlations of personal values with household expenditures as indicators of economic success (n= 293)

Value	All household goods	Luxuries of urban life (e.g. video)	Business inputs	Food of a balanced diet	Food of a traditional diet
Power	.07	.05	.02	-.35**	-.01
Achievement	.01	.00	.05	-.13*	.19*
Hedonism	.30**	.16**	.17**	-.25**	-.44**
Stimulation	.24**	.09	.21**	-.23**	-.26**
Self-direction	-.04	.08	.05	-.17**	.13*
Universalism	-.07	-.03	-.10	.20**	.14*
Benevolence	-.15*	-.04	-.02	.23**	.16**
Conformity	-.15*	-.05	-.20**	.20**	.20**
Security	-.17**	-.12*	-.20**	.14*	.18**
Tradition: self abnegation	-.04	-.08	-.04	.23**	-.15*
Tradition: customs and religion	-.01	.00	-.02	.19*	.12*

**p<0.01, *p<0.05

(one item refers to the 'needy in society') and improving standards of living in the community. Universalism values also enhance the motivation to gain skills and knowledge through joining projects. This follows from the emphasis of universalism values on intellectual openness – wisdom, broadmindedness, and tolerance.

We turn next to the relation of individual values to levels of performance in the projects. An indicator of escape from poverty to economic success is the level of household expenditure. This is the index of poverty preferred by the Uganda Bureau of Statistics. Respondents reported whether they had recently purchased the items on a list of specific household goods such as cutlery, clothes, sheets, furniture, radio cassette, video, and so on. They then reported whether they had purchased the items on a list of business inputs such as a boat, drier, sewing machine, pump, fishing nets, poultry equipment, and storeroom and farm tools. Finally, they reported how often they eat from a list of specific food items such as rice, meat, fish, millet, and so on, using a 5-point scale ranging from 'every day' to 'not at all'.

For purposes of analysis, we distinguished a luxury subset of household goods and two types of diet. A factor analysis of the food items indicated that a balanced diet composed of eggs, fish, chicken, rice, and potatoes could be discriminated from a traditional diet of millet, posho, and beans. Table 4.7 presents the correlations between personal values and the various expenditure indicators of economic success.

The most consistent and substantial correlations of the different categories of expenditure in Table 4.7 are with hedonism and stimulation values. Compared with others, individuals who emphasise these values spend a lot on household goods and business inputs. Not surprisingly, those who emphasise hedonism are particularly likely to buy luxury goods. On the other hand, they spend relatively less of their resources on food, spending especially little on a traditional diet. The expenditure pattern of these individuals suggests that they are relatively well off financially and are less traditional culturally.

Those who value security and conformity values exhibit a pattern of correlations with expenditures opposite to the pattern for those who value hedonism and stimulation. This finding is consistent with the opposition between openness and conservation values in the structural component of the values theory (Schwartz, 1992). Individuals for whom it is important to maintain secure, non-threatening, social and material environments are more frugal with their expenditures, perhaps because they wish to preserve their resources and be prepared against possibly threatening circumstances. These individuals also spend more of their resources on food, both traditional food and the set of foods that constitute a balanced diet. The overall pattern of expenditures suggests that those who emphasise conservation values are relatively more traditional and less well-to-do than others.

Finally, we examined relations of personal values to a set of indicators of the impact that participation in projects has on the individual's economic success. They include three indicators of successful growth of the project: (1) expansion of the employee base – the extent of increase in the number of non-family employees working on the project as compared with family members; (2) expansion of business—the extent of increase in numbers of customers for one's products and of stock to sell; (3) regularity of income from the project—the extent to which project activities yield regular income. Another set of indicators are the sources of income on which the individual relies to pay household bills, health bills, and school fees. To what extent has the project become the main source of income for participants, and to what extent do they rely on each of a variety of other sources?

Table 4.8 presents the correlations of personal value priorities with each of these indicators of project impact on economic success. Given the large number of correlations in this table, it is likely that some statistically significant results are nonetheless due to chance. We therefore refrain from trying to interpret those results whose meanings are not clear.

As a result of participating in the project, people who emphasise power values had increased the number of non-kin individuals they employ, as compared with family employees. Their orientation to gaining control over people and resources may have motivated them more than others to expand their employee base as a way to succeed in their project and increase wealth. In contrast, people who emphasise conformity and tradition values were less likely than others to expand their employee base. These values encourage people to comply with the expectations of close others and to submit themselves to accepted ways of doing things. Conformity and tradition values are likely to discourage project participants from going beyond the family circle to employ outsiders whose norms and expectations may be different. It is less clear why hedonism correlates positively with expanding the employee base beyond the family.

Individuals who attribute importance to power and security values had succeeded more than others in turning their projects into regular sources of income (column 3,

Table 4.8: Correlations of personal values with indicators of project impact on economic success (n= 293)

	Project growth				Sources of income			
	Increased non-kin employee	Increased customer base & stock	Regularity of income from project	Project partici-pation	Spouse's income	Other business involve-ment	Relat-ives	Wages from non-project work
Power	.19**	.03	.16*	.10	.10	-.03	-.09	-.15*
Achievement	.04	.12	-.03	-.02	.13	-.25**	-.04	-.02
Hedonism	.17*	.03	-.22**	-.16*	.00	-.13	-.08	.18*
Stimulation	.02	.03	-.07	-.08	-.01	.04	-.08	.17*
Self direction	-.01	.11	-.02	-.10	-.05	.02	-.03	-.05
Universalism	.03	-.16*	.12	.00	.06	-.01	.05	.02
Benevolence	.13	-.05	-.05	-.08	-.16*	.10	.09	.14*
Tradition	-.16*	-.09	-.00	.00	-.03	.02	.04	-.10
Conformity	-.21**	.09	.01	.20**	-.10	.06	.01	-.11
Security	.03	-.17*	.16*	.10	.09	.00	-.02	-.02

**p<0.01, *p<0.05

Table 4.8). As noted, for those who emphasise security values, this may reflect successful, cautious management. Those who emphasise power values such as wealth and authority, on the other hand, may succeed in increasing their income because of their more competitive, self-enhancing orientation.

Only eight of the fifty correlations between value priorities and sources of income are reliable. Those who emphasise hedonism values derive less of their incomes than others from development projects and more from the wages they receive for non-project work. This is consistent with the earlier sets of findings regarding hedonism. People high in hedonism values tend to be relatively well-off financially, hesitant to work hard in the projects themselves, and hence less likely to benefit from them. Those who value stimulation exhibit a similar, though weaker, set of characteristics.

Those who emphasise conformity values rely more on their project as a source of income than others do. Perhaps their commitment to playing by the rules and obeying norms and expectations constrains them to refrain from asking for or from accepting money from other sources. As a result, they must rely on the project to provide the necessary income. Other value priorities have little effect on whether project participants meet their needs by drawing on income from their projects.

Conclusions

In comparing Uganda's cultural value profile with other sub-Saharan African countries, as well as with donor countries from Europe, we discovered a shared Black African cultural profile that was highly consistent with qualitative descriptions of African culture by students of the continent. As compared with European donor countries and with much of the rest of the world, the African culture emphasises Hierarchy, Embeddedness and, perhaps, Mastery at the expense of Egalitarianism, Intellectual and Affective Autonomy and Harmony. Uganda showed a prototypical African cultural profile.

In the regions of Uganda we studied, we found that the districts from the Central region, the region most exposed to Western influences and most economically developed, show the most African cultural profile. This suggests that any Westernisation of cultural values has had little impact on the values of the respondents we interviewed. The districts from the West and North show very similar profiles, lower in both Hierarchy and Embeddedness and higher in Autonomy.

The last part of the chapter examined relations of individual differences in personal values to participation in development projects and to economic performance and success. For this purpose, we employed a theory of personal values that discriminate among individual persons.

The results indicate that personal values help to explain variations across people who join development projects, in their reasons for joining, in their household expenditures, and in some of the ways they organise the work on their projects and their success in deriving economic benefit from them. Many of the explanations also imply a causal influence of personal values on motives and behaviour.

There is a tendency to ignore the individual-in-development approach when promoting policies oriented towards poverty alleviation. Chapter Three presented the argument that this is often erroneous, because individuals undertake their tasks in embedded contexts we have referred to as cultural interfaces. The culturally patterned beliefs, values and practices of individuals are often not obvious, so it is important to search for and actively identify them in planning development projects.

In this chapter we identified several important cultural interfaces in sub-Saharan Africa that should be considered during policy making and policy implementation. A crucial component of all cultural interfaces is the basic values that underlie, rationalise, and justify people's behaviour. Values are relatively amenable to investigation and have attracted substantial research attention from academics. However, policy makers have had limited success in utilising the findings on values. This may be due to the difficulties involved in relating such findings to individual and group behaviour in projects. The last part of this chapter demonstrates that individual differences in values do relate to specific behaviours that may either assist individuals to escape from poverty or may make it difficult for them to do so.

If we recognise that these individual values are part of the cultural interfaces in which individuals behave, it becomes clear that these are culturally patterned values that guide individual decisions. Whatever the situation, individuals will tend to choose, rationalise and justify behaviour on the basis of the values they accept and reject. If the values they are prepared to accept and defend are in line with project objectives and practices, potential project beneficiaries or implementers are likely to be motivated to participate and promote the intended project objectives. If, on the other hand, these objectives and practices are grounded in values they are predisposed to ignore or reject, they are unlikely to co-operate in the implementation of the project on a sustainable basis.

---

1. The scores for Egalitarianism contradict this picture. We suspect, however, that the PVQ-based measurement of Egalitarianism is inadequate in these samples. The correlations of Egalitarianism with the other cultural values across districts are inconsistent with the theorised and observed patterns of intercorrelation among the other cultural value orientations. We therefore do not rely on the Egalitarianism scores for interpreting cultural differences among regions.

5
Networking: The Social Psychological Foundations of Development

In Chapter 3, we emphasised that the focus when considering poverty, escaping from poverty or development in general, should shift from end results, such as people's income, to the activities in which people actually engage. In this we were guided by Lev Semenovich Vygotsky, who recognised that to understand a product required focusing on the processes that produce it (Vygotsky, 1978, Wertsch, 1997). In studying a product, we merely describe it, whereas by investigating how it came to be, we can explain it. Vygotsky developed his ideas in opposition to psychological behaviourism and biological reductionism because he found these incomplete. He claimed that, by their very methods, they could not examine the dynamic aspects of their subject matter.

Granovetter (1985) made a related argument for the social sciences. He maintained that the study of social and economic behaviour and action has missed much of what takes place by assuming an over-socialised or an under-socialised individual. Some sociologists assume an over-socialised individual by treating the person as an android who blindly follows the norms, customs, and regulations of society. Many economists, in contrast, assume that the person is an under-socialised individual who follows the principle of maximising his or her personal utility. Granovetter argued that neither type of individual exists. Instead, the actions of real individuals are embedded in a prevailing context that leads sometimes to ignoring utility maximisation and sometimes to violating societal mores.

We build on these ideas in this chapter. We treat the person both as socialised and as a utility maximiser, depending on the context. We examine how people act within the context of their social networks, how they learn continuously from these networks and alter them. The chapter first examines the nature of social networks and networking. It then shows how development depends on networking. Finally, it presents and discusses data on how some Ugandan peasants who were attempting to escape poverty established and utilised networks and networking.

Cognitive development as the basis for community development

When studying development, how do we move from the individual, as a unit on which communities are based, to the collective or community itself? This transition is critical because our approach to understanding community poverty and efforts to escape it commits us to focusing on the individual actor. This standard problem of the transition from micro to macro has never been resolved fully (Granovetter, 1973, 1985). Nevertheless, pointers on how to proceed can be drawn from traditional disciplines, particularly from social psychology, which occupies a middle ground between micro and macro studies of society. Social psychology addresses issues at the intersection between the individual and the social: social influences on individual processes such as motivation, attribution, and learning; shared individual processes such as social attitudes and speech; group-based processes such as leadership, co-operation and competition, and enacting social roles. The premises, theories, constructs, and methodologies of social psychology guide us in this chapter.

Granovetter (1973) suggested that interpersonal relations or interpersonal networks, as he refers to them, provide the basis for macro-level development. This is a useful link between the micro and macro as it relates to development and escaping from poverty. Interpersonal networks are small-scale interactions that translate into large-scale patterns (Granovetter, 1973: p. 1360) which then find their way back into interpersonal networks. Early studies examined networks built around focal individuals or subsumed within organisations. Granovetter departed from this approach by identifying networks that are based on issues as the focus of study. In this spirit, we study networks whose objective is to cope with poverty and escape from it. To prepare the ground for studying poverty-focused networks, we discuss a generalised network we refer to as a learning network. Learning networks are a good starting point for examining poverty because, we postulate, sustainable development begins with cognitive development, that is, learning new ways of looking at (perceiving), thinking about, analysing and storing events, making, implementing, and evaluating decisions and policies (Vygotsky, 1978).

Three models of community learning

The most elaborate model of community learning is the zone of proximal development (Vygotsky, 1978). This advocates a network understanding of development but does not use the prevailing language of networks. We will begin our discussion with this model. Second is the weak bridges framework (Granovetter, 1973); and third is the structural hole model (Burt, 1997). The last two models are closely related and derive directly from studies of the influence of networks on community development. All three models implicitly assume a central principle of social learning, namely, that learning takes place through reciprocal interaction with the social context (Lewin, 1946, quoted in Shaw & Constanzo, 1970; Bandura, 1978).

Vygotsky's theory of cognitive development and the zone of proximal development

Vygotsky suggested distinguishing between simple and complex behaviour or, in his words, low-level and higher-level mental functions, when studying development. Simple behaviour or low-level mental functions include such primary cognitive processes as thinking, memory, perception, and attention. Such behaviour is instinctive and responds to changes in the stimulus environment. Complex or higher-level functions include verbal thought and reasoning, logical memory, and selective attention. In Vygotsky's schema, development takes place when an individual or a group of individuals achieve higher-level mental functions. These are controlled reather than instinctive functions, deployed by the individual or community at will.

To illustrate these levels of functioning, consider reactions to a burning bush. Using only lower-level functions, a person or animal would react by running away. Relying on higher-level functions, a person might treat the fire as a way to get rid of refuse, as an opportunity for celebrating at a bonfire, or to cook. The behaviour of a mother in feeding her baby can also illustrate different levels of functioning. The child's crying signals the mother to feed her, a simple environmental stimulus setting off the lower-level functions of memory. In contrast, the mother may work out a regular feeding schedule and record in her diary the exact times of feedings. When the time for a feeding arrives, the mother will feed her baby even before it cries. Here the mother, rather than the stimulus environment, controls her behaviour using logical memory.

It is in the nature of higher-level mental functions that their application varies from community to community. Take, for example, selective attention: people pay attention to events that are meaningful to them and ignore those that are not. But what is defined as meaningful is defined at least in part by the specific socio-cultural context. Because the application of higher-level mental functions is situation specific, Vygotsky also referred to them as cultural functions. People attend to what their culture conditions them to attend to. Thus Vygotsky's theory of development relies on both social and cultural learning.

Vygotsky specified three inter-related factors that influence learning of higher-mental functions or cultural functions. First, is prior experience or history; second is interpersonal activity or activity carried out with one's superiors or peers; third are the tools such as language, gestures and material technology used in carrying out activities. All three factors are situation specific. Each factor points to a method or process for understanding and explaining how development occurs (Wertsch, 1997). First, one should examine the historical and or developmental experience of the unit of study (individual or community). Second, one should examine the social processes through which cultural functioning or higher mental functions arise. Third, one should study the tools and signs that mediate among the mental processes. These three core processes underlie Vygotsky's departure from many social learning psychologists and developmentalists. He asserts:

> We need to concentrate not on the product of development but on the very process by which higher forms are established....To encompass in research the process or a given thing's development in all its phases and changes – from birth to death – fundamentally means to discover its nature, its essence, for it is only in movement that a body shows what it is. Thus, the historical [that is, in the broadest sense of history] study of behaviour is not an auxiliary aspect of theoretical study, but rather forms its very base (Vygotsky, 1978, pp 64-65).

Vygotsky's three core processes articulate the interactional nature of development in general and of cognitive development, specifically. A further distinction between interpersonal and intrapersonal learning underlines the role of interactions in the process of development. Interpersonal learning takes place through collaboration in activities with one's peers and superiors or through instruction. In intrapersonal learning, individuals fit what they have learned from interpersonal contacts into their own mental schemas. During this stage in development, learning acquired socially is internalised and the individual becomes acculturated. Acculturated persons are able to use their new knowledge without help and to modify that knowledge depending on their own circumstances. Acculturated persons become agents who help others to learn as they participate jointly in activities. Thus, as Granovetter (1973) suggested, small-scale interactions can have large scale effects at the community level.

In order to understand intrapersonal learning, it is essential to understand the interpersonal learning that preceded it. In what tasks did the learner participate and with whom? The answers to such developmental/historical questions help to explain the level and quality of learning and acculturation an individual exhibits. Since learning occurs through joint activities or instruction, it is also necessary to identify the tools used to transmit knowledge, especially the communication tools.

The above discussion emphasises that human cognitive development is a product of the inter-relationship between the individual and society. Individuals notice and attribute meanings to objects and events that are significant and meaningful to those around them. Vygotsky further elaborated his ideas about the social origins of higher mental functioning with the concept of *zones of proximal development*. This is the distance between the level of development people actually attain based on independent problem solving and the level they could potentially attain through problem solving under adult guidance or in collaboration with more capable peers, (Vygotsky, 1978; Wertsch, 1997). Because people are embedded in social relations, what they could attain with the assistance of others is, in a sense, even more indicative of their mental development than what they can do alone.

The interpersonal learning and development that takes place in the zone of proximal development follows three stages: First collaborators pay close attention to each other and maintain their attention. Second, they work in step or practise their collaborative activity, working at the same pace. Third, they work more independently but co-ordinate their activities through communication (Wertsch, 1997).

The concept of zones of proximal development implies that interpersonal learning occurs only when there is potential for growth within a person's network of social relations. Thus the zone of proximal development sets the limits for growth. However, the zone may atrophy and no longer constitute a network with resources for learning. In this case, interpersonal learning or development by the individual or community ceases and stagnation sets in. This happens when people can find no new collaborative activity from which to learn, as when all collaborative activity repeats the same routines. It is at this point that the zone of proximal development for a particular individual or community begins to degenerate. Of course, newcomers will find the same activities novel and they will develop their mental capacities up to learning boundaries set by the zone. To stop such decay, the zone of proximal development must be rejuvenated or revitalised. We next discuss how this can occur.

Structural holes, weak bridges and personal initiative

The development of a community correlates positively with the number of associations in the community (Putnam, 1993). From our viewpoint, associations provide zones of proximal development in which people can collaborate with others or receive instruction. Burt (1997) built on Putnam's ideas by proposing that communities that do not have a number of discrete associations or networks will stagnate. He conceives of communities or social structures as made up numerous discrete networks, each of which enjoys resources that are unique either in quality or degree. He refers to the gap (distance) between one network and another as a structural hole. The more structural holes in a society or community, the more likely it is to develop and to avoid stagnation or decay. But the gaps between networks or associations must be spanned in order to rejuvenate the zones of proximal development. For this to occur, one or more individuals must hold membership in multiple associations. Strong ties among members of an association serve to institutionalise values within a particular network or zone of proximal development (see Figure 5.1, on p.88). Weak ties help to transmit new values and knowledge to other networks. We elaborate on the strength of the ties found in networks below.

The strength of interpersonal ties refers to the amount of time people spend together and to their levels of emotional intensity, mutual confiding, and reciprocity. People with strong interpersonal ties tend to like and dislike the same people and things and to share similar values. Such mutually compatible sentiments and attitudes are psychologically balanced and comfortable (Heider, 1958). Strong ties are part of dense networks of relations in which everyone knows everyone else. Such networks are effective for institutionalising and socialising norms and values (Noble, 1973), but they do not promote change. Granovetter (1973) argues that strong ties are less productive of innovation, adaptability, and diffusion of ideas than weak ties.

Weak ties are parts of extended networks in which individuals meet occasionally with acquaintances but are not highly involved with them. Such acquaintances have their own strong ties elsewhere. Occasional contacts with those linked to other networks can bring fresh views from the other networks, raise new issues and suggest new ideas. Hence, extended networks that are bridged by weak ties are more effective for introducing new and innovative ideas to the community. Weak bridges to other networks can rejuvenate an otherwise atrophying zone of proximal development. Granovetter (1973) illustrated the greater influence of weak bridges in a study of how people found new jobs. Successful job seekers were those who got tips from acquaintances outside their immediate circles who knew of vacancies. The key was the weak bridge with access to different information not available within the dense network of close friends.[1]

The idea that people have a zone of proximal development highlights the fact that people's strong ties form networks that provide the context for learning and development but also set boundaries for such learning. Strong networks of people with whom one is close and in direct and constant contact are influential in creating norms and values, but they are inadequate for continued adaptive learning and growth. These require societies to possess numerous weakly linked zones of proximal development that constitute extended networks. The weak bridges among these extended networks prevent fragmentation of society into cliques of independent, high-density, strong networks that prevent social cohesion and the diffusion of ideas. Strong networks that are not linked by weak bridges are unable to mobilise to cope with external threats. For example, consider the responses of Uganda, Kenya, and Tanzania to the invasion of Lake Victoria by the water hyacinth. This invasion threatened the livelihoods of their fishermen by destroying shallow water fish (e.g., tilapia). Each country acted as a strong, independent network that could not link up with the others to develop shared solutions to this invasion. They lacked the weak bridges needed to mobilise for the joint effort required to solve the problem.

Burt (1997) describes the process of weak ties in terms of bridging the structural holes between networks. When networks reach the limits of the resources available within their own zone of proximal development, they require information that may be found in other networks in order to continue to learn and solve problems. If a member of one network has a footing in another network, he or she may be able to transfer knowledge across the structural hole. Success in transferring knowledge depends, however, on the climate of freedom within the networks that permits or interferes with the actions of those who might serve as bridges (Rotter & Hochreich, 1975). The hierarchy of authority and the rules that prevail in a network grant some individuals legitimacy to engage in bridging but not others. Moreover, the presence of peers with alternative ideas creates competition for influence. Hence, potential bridging persons must establish their legitimacy before their new ideas will be taken seriously. To examine just what bridging persons (or bridges) do to establish legitimacy we review briefly a recent model of personal initiative that has also been used successfully in African researches (Freze, 2000). We select this model because of its emphasis on action, the paradigm we prefer.

According to Frese and Zapf (1994), action is goal-oriented behaviour that is organised in specific ways by goals, information integration, plans, and feedback. Action can be regulated consciously or via routines. Frese and Zapf (1994) argue that the concept of goal integrates motivational and cognitive concepts. In the action process, an action proceeds from a goal to a plan to its execution and to feedback. The concept of goal implies, in addition, persistence in spite of barriers and setbacks and tenacity in pursuit of objectives, when confronted with difficult situations. In this process personal initiative, risk taking, and innovativeness are crucial. Personal initiative is a proactive behaviour syndrome expressed in taking an active and self-starting approach to work and going beyond what is formally required in a situation. It is directed toward the individual's goals and maintained in the long term in the face of barriers and setbacks (Frese, et al, 1996, p. 38). Innovation, on the other hand, is a social process that combines generating new ideas with involving others in implementing these ideas. A person can be creative and generate new ideas alone, but the implementation of ideas typically depends upon the approval, support and resources of others. Taking personal initiatives and introducing innovations involves risk, as both processes entail deviation from the norm.

Learning to escape from poverty: An empirical study

The models put forward above argue forcefully that learning and development are more a product of interaction than of action. This literature stands in opposition to structural func-tionalism, with its focus on the functions of static structures. The network literature treats structures as dynamic entities with indefinite boundaries that undergo constant change in response to their internal and external environments (Johnston & Lawrence, 1998; Knoke & Kuklinski, 1998, Willis, 1994). The remainder of this chapter applies the ideas presented above to examine the efforts of a number of villagers to escape poverty. These villagers

Figure 5.1: The zone of proximal development (Adapted from Kepfrener, 1973 and Vygotsky, 1978)

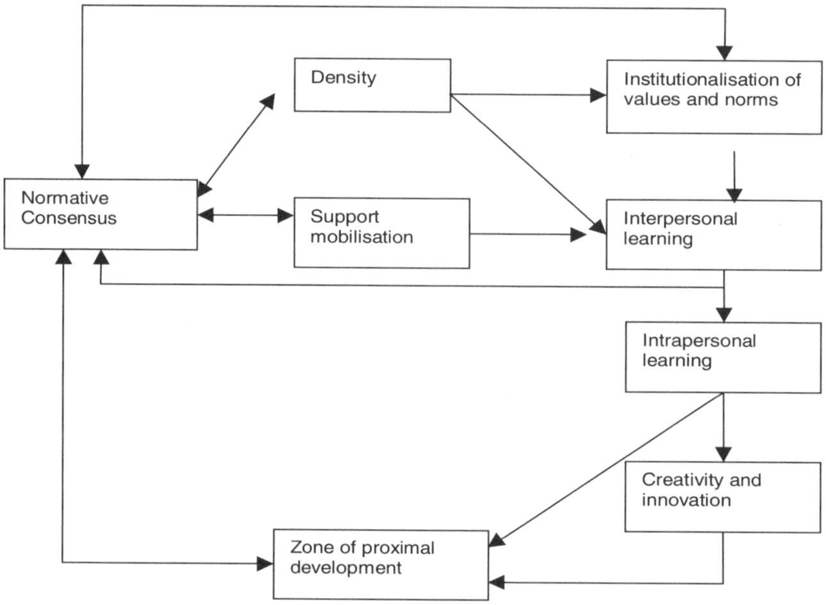

experienced poverty in the form of insecurity regarding food and other basic household necessities. We examine qualitative data that reveals the processes of networking that the villagers employed and the roles they played in the networks as they attempted to escape from poverty. Figure 5.1 provides a conceptual map of the ideas we use to guide our analysis of the villagers' efforts and their outcomes. It makes explicit the links between aspects of the processes of learning and development in networks. Each link represents a proposition about the nature of these processes.

The qualitative data on which we base the analyses are case studies, arrayed in a matrix (Miles & Huberman, 1994). We employ event listing and role matrix formats in order to capture the content and relational aspect of the networks the villagers used to escape poverty.

Proposition 1: The zone of proximal development is associated with normative consensus.

The case of a group of villagers living in a village 20 kilometres north of Kampala illustrates this proposition. These villagers experienced perennial food shortages and insecurity because the rocky landscape with saline topsoil that they farmed on was infertile. For unknown reasons, the village had never utilised the services of an agricultural extension worker to show them how to overcome this problem. Over time,

Case study 5.1: Respondent 36's narrative

CASE NO: 36

DISTRICT: MPIGI

SUB COUNTY: GOMBE

VILLAGE: LWADDA

PROJECT: TWEGOMBE WOMEN'S ASSOCIATION

Q. HOW DID YOU JOIN THIS PROJECT?

I am a native of Lwadda. From time immemorial Lwadda has suffered from poor crop yields because of poor soil in the area. When a certain family settled in the village, they began growing crops but, unlike the natives of Lwadda, this family got better yields. I and many other people in the village began wondering why. The new settlers became the talk of the village and even of neighbouring villages. People asked themselves what that woman (Hajati Kalema) was doing to her crops. Some superstitious people even went as far as saying she had supernatural powers that enabled her to get better crop yields and to successfully produce some crops that others had failed with. Others said the new settlers had been banned from their place of origin because of the supernatural powers they possessed.

However, I did not think this way. I believed that Hajati had better methods of agriculture, and I wanted to learn them. Therefore, I decided to make friends with the newcomer and to become close to her, knowing I would eventually learn the secret behind Hajati's exceptionally high yields. I succeeded in my plan. I befriended Hajati, who gathered four other women in the village and formed an association known as Twegombe Women's Association. Hajati taught us sustainable methods of agriculture. With this aid, we improved our farming and got yields similar to those of Hajati. Later, other women also joined, and Hajati taught them better farming methods too.

they had come to believe that it was impossible to get good harvests in their village and they were suspicious of anyone who claimed it could be done. As Case Study 5.1 indicates, this is exactly how they reacted when a settler knowledgeable in dealing with saline soil came into their midst.

In this case, the village was a zone of proximal development where villagers had exhausted their own resources and lacked the knowledge to surmount the problem of poor yields. They could not develop further without acquiring knowledge from an external source. But they were unwilling to accept such knowledge. Indeed, they had concluded that it was not possible to expect significant harvests from farming efforts in their village and had ceased trying. When a newcomer arrived and disproved these expectations, they expressed their normative consensus spontaneously: Most villagers rejected the newcomer, making her the talk of the village and expressing negative evaluations (supernatural powers, banning from her own village). Although the zone of proximal development in the village had atrophied, most villagers were unprepared to seek or to accept knowledge from a woman who could serve as a bridge to other networks. Instead, the newcomer's innovative and progressive ideas aroused fears

Case study 5.2: Founding a community-based association

CASE NO: 60 = Hajati Kalema
DISTRICT: MPIGI
SUBCOUNTY: GOMBE
VILLAGE: LWADDA
NAME OF PROJECT: TWEGOMBE WOMEN'S DEVELOPMENT ASSOCIATION.

Q. WHY DID YOU FOUND TWEGOMBE?

After the 1986 Museveni War, I settled in the village - Lwadda B, and found the people of the village to be neither hardworking nor progressive. They were not interested in good things. They had no ambition (*baali tebegomba*) and had no admiration for those who were successful. Instead, they felt envious over small things. To reduce the evil feelings, I realised that I had to bring people close to me and persuade them to do similar things to what I was doing.

Before I migrated to Lwadda B, I had been an active member of Environmental Alert where I had acquired skills. In 1992, I gathered five women together and we formed a small group of six people called Twegombe Women's Association. This group comprised women engaged in animal husbandry and crop farming. We had the following objectives:

• To develop one another's family
• To promote women's income generating activities
• To teach women how to use money. Some women were getting money but did not know how to use it.
• To teach women to grow such things like matooke and vegetables using locally made manure and using the environment sustainably.
• To promote good feeding and to ensure food security for participants' families.

With time, women around heard and saw what members of Twegombe were doing and they gradually joined one by one. By 1994, there were 16 members and now there are 25 members. The name Twegombe (let us be ambitious) arose out of the need to develop an admiring spirit among members so that they could learn to admire other people's good work and in the process strive to attain similar achievements.

that were shared widely by most of the members of her adopted village. The normative consensus in the village was growth negative.

As the respondent told us however, a few women were privately interested in the new ideas. They wished to 'revitalise their zone of proximal development'. The interview with the newcomer herself demonstrates this positive side of networking.

Hajati Kalema gathered half a dozen women around her who had a common interest in crop farming and animal husbandry. They agreed on the purposes of their network of relations and directed their new knowledge and skills to solving immediate existential problems. The purposes they pursued ranged from sustainable agriculture to management of savings and to good neighbourliness.

This case study illustrates the two sides of the zone of proximal development and its associations with normative consensus. The village farmers of Lwadda had reached the limit of their zone of proximal development; they could not continue on the way they were going if they were to overcome their food insecurity. The newcomer came to the conclusion that the inhabitants of her adopted village did not know how to work with poor soils, how to manage their finances, and how to live peacefully together. Both the woman villager and the newcomer gave similar interpretations of what was transpiring in the village, providing a basis for forming a fresh normative consensus about what to do. The woman villager sought to overcome the limits of the atrophied zone of proximal development in the village by befriending the person with the knowledge needed to progress. The newcomer, on the other hand, decided to create a new zone of proximal development in which new development knowledge could be imparted to her adopted village.

The responses of the newcomer, Hajati Kalema, clarify how a zone of proximal development can lead to actual development. The newcomer built a new network of friends and collaborators. They generated their own zone of proximal development in which new resources were exploited and interpersonal learning took place. They also formed a new normative consensus and institutionalised a set of values and norms different from those that had formerly dominated in the village. Another important fact comes through in this analysis: the changes first took place at the cognitive level of the members of the host community. This supports Vygotsky's contention that development begins at the cognitive level and spreads to other levels such as the material and the attitudinal.

Proposition 2: Normative consensus is associated with density and support mobilisation.

This proposition asserts that when people develop a normative consensus by agreeing on what to do, they then tend to increase the frequency and intensity of their interaction (*density*) and to seek support for their viewpoint from others (*mobilisation*). As noted, the villagers had developed a normative consensus about the impossibility of successfully raising crops on their land and about the pointlessness of trying. This consensus led to an increased intensity and frequency of interaction among them when challenged by the newcomer's success. People met more often, spoke more, and generated shared explanations of what was happening, of the need to reject the newcomer, and of how to discredit her activities. They mobilised support from one another for this interpretation of the situation.

On the other side, the development of divergent normative consensus and support mobilisation evolved largely from joint activity by the villager who had befriended the newcomer, the newcomer herself, and, subsequently, other village women. The divergent normative consensus emerged as a result of planning based on self-interest. Thus a person who admired the newcomer sought her out in order to learn her methods and to exploit them to solve her own food shortage. Hajati Kalema also purposefully stage-managed the generation of consensus by bringing together women she thought would share her interests. This was made easier by one of the villagers seeking her out and

Case study 5.3: Institutionalising values and norms through density and interpersonal learning

CASE NO: 62

DISTRICT: MPIGI

SUBCOUNTY: GOMBE

VILLAGE: LWADDA A

NAME OF PROJECT: TWEGOMBE WOMEN'S DEVELOPMENT ASSOCIATION

Q. WHY DID YOU JOIN?

I migrated from Rubaga and settled in Lwadda A village in 1993. I had a sister-in-law who was a member of Twegombe and was staying near Hajati (Kalema) the founder of Twegombe Women's Association. Whenever I visited that in-law, I would find women gathered there and would wonder what the gatherings were all about.

One day I asked my sister-in-law and she explained what Twegombe was doing and what it was all about. One time, when I was at my sister-in-law's place, I met Hajati there and was invited to join Twegombe. At that time, Twegombe was mostly engaged in agricultural activities, and I was not interested in agriculture at all and thought I could not manage it. My sister-in-law's husband also held a similar view that I would not manage agriculture because it involves a lot of tiresome work. However, I was interested in co-operative work and I had engaged in Co-op work before migrating from Rubaga.

On another occasion, I visited Hajati, who gave me more details about Twegombe. I still thought I could not manage that kind of work. I also thought that the project required a very big piece of land and my land was just one acre with very poor saline soil. I imagined that growing crops on that kind of soil was a waste of time. Thus, since the project basically dealt with agriculture at that time, I thought I did not have the requirements. However, I went ahead and paid the membership fee of Shs 2,000/= $2 and also paid the contribution of Shs 10,000/= $10 for the association in December 1994, although I remained inactive. Meanwhile, I became a member of another women's association in the area, one that engaged in singing, an area that greatly interested me. Later, this association moved to Rock View Matugga, far away from where I lived. Members of this association were not very active and they tended to come late, making it difficult for me to get back home.

In 1995, Hajati approached me again and asked why I was not active in the Twegombe association even though I had paid all the required fees. At this point, I gave up my membership in the other women's association and started being active in Twegombe. I undertook training in making a vegetable garden. Making these gardens is a very difficult work. If one is not determined, one can easily give up. For instance, you need to make composite manure for a vegetable garden, but I did not have an animal to provide the dung for making manure. So I collected cow dung from Hajati and from another lady in the village. I started with a vegetable garden of nakati, a spinach-like vegetable with rough leaves. This garden gave such a good yield that I was encouraged to make a second garden for cabbage and a third for tomatoes. These gardens saved me a daily expense of Shs.2,000 needed to buy vegetables.

In addition, Hajati was a very good person who sometimes gave members seedlings. She also shopped around for experts to train members of Twegombe in various skills and to inspect their work. Although I had hated farming initially, this inspired me to engage more in agricultural work. My land lies on a steep hill, so I was taught how to make ridges (*ensalosalo*) to prevent soil erosion.

Hajati also encouraged members to grow elephant grass. Having such grass would enable one to raise a heifer, if a donor could be found to provide a heifer. Although I did not own a cow, I decided to grow elephant grass because I also saw that women who had cows would take the grass in exchange for milk. Hajati also advised me to use the elephant grass for mulching my banana trees. When I did this, the trees gave a good harvest. This inspired me to do even more farming.

wanting to learn from her. As the group worked together, the density of their interaction increased and they sought support from the village for the new ways of crop farming. Indeed, they even sought support in neighbouring villages.

Proposition 3: Density is associated with support mobilisation, interpersonal learning, and institutionalisation of values and norms

We have just illustrated the relationship between density and support mobilisation. The next case study provides examples of how density can relate to the institutionalisation of values and norms and to interpersonal learning or learning through co-activity.

This third case describes how a person was gradually drawn into a new network, became involved in dense interaction with its members, accepted the values and normative consensus of that network, acquired from it skills previously unavailable to her, and used it as a zone of proximal development to help solve her everyday problems. Moreover, her success in new activities increased her self-regard and willingness to take initiatives. The first steps were driven by chance and curiosity. Initially there were visits to her sister-in-law's home where she happened to see women meeting and wondered about what was going on. Later steps were voluntarily guided by her own desire to work in groups (what she called co-operative activities) and, subsequently, to improve her standard of living. Lastly came Hajati's careful cultivation and mobilisation of support.

Central to this whole process was interpersonal learning of farming and other skills from Hajati and others. As described by Vygotsky, the enduring attributes that enabled this woman to become a successful farmer were acquired through a process of interpersonal learning through concrete observation and instruction. Learning of farming skills was achieved by observing exactly how mulching is done, how composite manure is made, and how ridges are made on a hilly landscape to avoid soil erosion. In addition, the woman in this case study learned how to co-operate peacefully and profitably with her neighbours. She learned to exchange the elephant grass she planted for milk from neighbours who wanted the grass for their own cows.

This case also illustrates how values and norms regarding crop farming were institutionalised in the village. Hajati Kalema brought to the village values of co-operative work, the capacity to draw on and to learn from experts outside one's immediate acquaintances, and to adopt norms of farming in particular successful ways. However, she had to build a network of women who would work together in order to institutionalise these values and norms and mobilise support for them in the village. First, she had to overcome the potential participants' belief that farming could not succeed. Second, she had also to change their low self-opinions as crop farmers. She performed these through demonstrating her own success and instructing the village women in successful farming. In Case Study 5.3, Hajati managed to draw a participant into the network on the basis of motivations unrelated to the core farming agenda of the network—her desire to spend time and co-operate with other women. Repeated encounters providing ever more dense interaction combined with the respondent's own disposition towards co-operative work to make her an active member of the crop and animal husbandry network known as Twegombe.

We have described activities of three persons involved in the Twegombe Women's Association. Table 5.1 summarises the formation of this community-based organisation, founded to solve specific problems that were rooted in an atrophying zone of proximal development. The table is a role matrix that indicates the role of some of the people who joined Twegombe at its foundation. It also illustrates a number of the relationships and propositions in the model from Table 5.2. It demonstrates that networking and networks are expressed as a series of individual activities that focus on identifiable, specific areas of activity.

The three case studies discussed above demonstrated the centrality of learning activity in a development network or what we refer to as a zone of proximal development. The women's learning and development show that Twegombe served as a zone of proximal development. Table 5.1 illustrates various propositions and constructs relevant for analysing networks, using more case studies from this project. Cases 60, 36, and 62 point to instances of normative consensus, density of interaction and support mobilisation. They also demonstrate the interrelations among these elements and the institutionalisation of values, norms and interpersonal learning. Mobilisation of support is well-illustrated by cases 37 and 31. Hajati Kalema, the focal individual in this network, first mobilised support by turning to her neighbour (37). The latter then joined the mobilisation effort by recruiting another volunteer. In case 31, mobilisation followed involvement in interaction with the network. Only after observing the activities of a group of people at Hajati Kalema's homestead was this woman mobilised to join. Hajati Kalema initiated the dynamics we have described. The resources she used for this purpose were also a product of interpersonal learning. Note that she had been part of Environmental Alert before migrating to Lwadda. She had internalised what she learned in that network and put it to her own unique use by creating Twegombe. She demonstrated the three personal characteristics of a bridge as cited above. She showed personal initiative, innovativeness, and she took risks. In this way, she created or revitalised a zone of proximal development that provided new learning opportunities which members of this zone were able to utilise to solve initially insoluble problems. Table 5.2 summarises the revitalised zone we refer to as Lwadda Twegombe Zone of Proximal Development.

The left side of Table 5.2 describes the atrophied zone of development in Lwadda.

Table 5.1: Networking in the formation of Twegombe Women's Project

Case	Event 1	Event 2	Event 3	Event 4	Event 5	Event 6
60 (Hajati Kalema: HK)	Joined Environmental Alert.	Moved to Lwadda and practised crop farming skills acquired in Environmental Alert.	Formed Twegombe with 5 others to help poor families and women in 1992.	Taught members skills learned from Environmental Alert.	Twegombe grew to 16 members by 1994.	Numbers grew to 26 by 1997.
37	HK's neighbour who admired her crops.	HK approached her to form an association and to explain its advantages.	HK asked her to bring a volunteer	HK brought 4 other volunteers and formed Twegombe with 6 volunteers	HK trained the volunteers in modern agricultural methods	Twegombe grew to 25 volunteers. HK found various trainers.
36	Observed a new household settle in Lwadda in 1987, soon after the civil war.	Observed success of this household, headed by HJ in crop farming with outstanding yields.	Engaged with villagers in talk about new settlers because all other families had low yields.	Visited HK in order to befriend her and learn her secrets.	Welcomed by HK who explained what she does.	They form a new association in 1992.
62	Migrated from Rubaga to Lwadda.	Visited sister-in-law, found women gathered, inquired what they were doing.	Met HK who asked her to join Twegombe.	Was sceptical about her ability to crop farm successfully.	Paid dues but remained inactive	Approached by HK again. Joined, learned farming and used cow dung for manure.
31	Observed women learning new activities from HK.	Husband too sick for her to join Twegombe even though she desired to.	Derived income from 2 cows her husband was responsible for.	Sold one cow to treat husband who nevertheless passed away.	Approached by HK to join.	Joined to learn how to look after the remaining cow and other activities.

Table 5.2: Lwadda-Twegombe zone of proximal development

Atrophying zone of proximal development			Revitalised zone of proximal development	
Village and individual constraints	Underlying causes	Coping before Twegombe	Solution after Twegombe	Outcome
Poor soil	Known crop farming methods fail.	Reduce time spent in agricultural work.	Join association learn to improve land fertility.	Improved soil fertility.
Rocky terrain	Insufficient land to raise crops.	Reduce time spent in agricultural.	Join association: learn cultivation of rocky terrain.	More land available for agriculture.
Lack of motivation and laziness	Repeated failure to obtain good agricultural yields.	Reduce time doing agricultural work.	Spend more time doing agricultural work.	Improved agricultural yields.

The right side of Table 5.2 describes the revitalisation of this zone through the Twegombe community-based association. Hajati Kalema, the newcomer, quickly identified weaknesses in the community ranging from lack of knowledge to poor neighbourliness. She mobilised villagers to form an association through which they could learn how to solve their local problems. The association achieved considerable success and attracted people from neighbouring villages who came to learn from it and especially from its founder. This intervention created a revitalised zone of proximal development in which interpersonal learning could take place. The revitalised zone of proximal development became a source of learning for the wider community, as described in Case Study 5.4 on the next page and summarised in Table 5.2

Proposition 4: Interpersonal learning leads to intrapersonal learning.
The discussion of this proposition focuses on the cases of people from other villages that were experiencing problems similar to those that had led to the formation of Twegombe. They came to observe Twegombe, learned what to do, and initiated similar associations in their own villages.

This case emphasises the role of interpersonal learning and how it leads to intrapersonal learning. It also shows how micro-changes are translated into macro-development. By watching Hajati Kalema, the visitors from other villages learned how to create composite manure and use it to get maximum crop yields from small plots. The visitors also learned that it was possible to turn this type of agriculture into a viable business. They then internalised this learning and customised it to fit their own circumstances.

Case Study 5.4: From interpersonal to intrapersonal learning

CASE NO: 35

DISTRICT: Mpigi

SUB-COUNTY: Sisa

VILLAGE: Kitende

PROJECT: Akutwala Rural Development Association (ARDA)

Q. HOW DID YOU JOIN?

I was interested in agriculture all along. I used to see how women peasant farmers in my village grew crops, sold the good and big ones but ate the small or bad ones. I hated this practice because I always wanted to eat good things, particularly those I had grown. I felt that I should be able to raise only good crops both for myself and for the market.

One day a family friend, Mr Kikonyogo, visited a lady called Hajati Kalema of Twegombe Women's Association in Matugga. He was very impressed with Hajati's work and it inspired him to engage in agriculture and animal husbandry. When he returned, he told me how Hajati was using sustainable agriculture and locally made manure to get bumper harvests. He commented: We waste time going to Kampala to look for money when we leave the money in our homes. He meant that people have plenty of resources at home that they could utilise to become rich instead of going to Kampala to look for jobs.

Mr Kikonyogo arranged for me to visit Hajati. On the day of the visit, when we approached Hajati's home, I noticed a very big difference between Hajati's plants and those of her neighbours. It seemed as if the soil in Hajati's gardens had been brought from somewhere else. Everything I saw at Hajati's place was of great inspiration to me. When I returned home, I told my husband and other people about the good methods of farming and I escorted them on a visit to see for themselves. When we returned to our village, we informed other people about sustainable agriculture and soil conservation methods and we mobilised them to form an association (ARDA). The association started its activities by visiting people engaged in sustainable agriculture and animal husbandry. We strongly believed that if members saw successful examples of what other people were doing, they would be inspired to do similar things.

As further evidence that intrapersonal learning had occurred, they founded their own association and took their own initiatives to acquire knowledge from other sources.

Thus they altered and revitalised their own zones of proximal development as a vehicle for moving out of poverty. Table 5.3 spells out the process of formation of this association in an historical event matrix describing events in the life of the early members of ARDA. Case 34 in the Table is of particular relevance to the proposition that interpersonal learning leads to intrapersonal learning. This is the case in which an elderly man learned enough from Hajati Kalema to train the respondent in similar skills. The elderly man would not have been able to teach others if he had not internalised the learning he had acquired interpersonally. Another interesting aspect of this case is that the man tried to persuade the widow to give up trading in Kampala in favour of

Table 5.3: The formation of Akutwala Rural Development Association (ARDA)

Case	Event 1	Event 2	Event 3	Event 4	Event 5	Event 6
33	Mrs Mbaziira visited Hajati Kalema in Maatugga, returned home and co-founded ARDA.	She approached him to join ARDA in order to learn sustainable agriculture.	He was reluctant because he thought agriculture was all feminine work.	Eventually he was persuaded to try animal husbandry, an aspect ARDA also	He bought a cow which produced poor yields	He then joined ARDA to learn animal husbandry. ARDA invited Vision 2000 to train its members including him.
34	Worked as a trader in Kampala and was a widow.	She was approached by an elderly man from ARDA.	He asked her to join ARDA since working at home would be more profitable than trading in Kampala.	She was sceptical at first but joined anyway.	The elderly man taught her what he had learned in ARDA.	He arranged for UNDP trainers to provide training. Convinced by the training, which gave her a direction, she gave up trade.
35	A family friend visited Hajati Kalema of Twegombe.	The friend learned how Hajati used locally made manure to get good yields.	Friend arranged for her to visit Hajati Kalema.	She too mobilised others, including her husband to see for themselves.	When they return, they form their own association: ARDA.	
53	A friend joined ARDA and learned new ways of crop farming.	The friend invited her to join ARDA in order for her to learn the same.	She had many children she could not feed.	Her husband was not earning enough either.	She joined ARDA and learned new methods of agriculture.	Her harvests improved so she had food to spare. and to sell to the market.

agriculture. This was a big decision both for him and for the widow. Petty trading is generally known to be more profitable than farming. Most people would go into trading if they had enough capital to spare, as recent work on women in African economies has demonstrated (Snyder, 2000). However, the elderly man had first to alter the zone of proximal development for the widow before persuading her to give up petty trade. He did this by providing training in agriculture and by helping to bring UNDP experts to ARDA who could offer further training. In the complete narrative of her experience, the widow states that the training she received helped give her a new vision and mission in life. She became a successful horticultural farmer and gave up her daily trip to Kampala to engage in petty trade.

Proposition 5: Intrapersonal learning is associated with creativity, innovation and the creation of a new zone of proximal development.

Intrapersonal learning, referred to by Vygotsky (1978) as cultural learning or attaining higher mental functioning, is the key to *sustained* development of individuals and their communities. Whereas interpersonal learning brings understanding of *how* things happen, intrapersonal learning brings understanding of *why* they happen (Argyris, 1969). When people understand the 'why' of events, they are able to innovate creatively. Individuals with this ability can change the decaying or less than optimum zones of proximal development in their society and help the community to surmount the problems that have blocked development.

The cases discussed above provide many examples of innovation, based on intrapersonal learning that helped communities by creating new zones of proximal development. Most prominent was Hajati Kalema, who used her knowledge to create programmes of learning that taught management of household income, good neighbourliness, horticulture, and marketing horticulture produce. These contributed to the escape of many community members from poverty. A second example is the elderly man from ARDA, in Case 34. He drew on his knowledge to create a zone of proximal development for a widow that enabled her to acquire skills, change her self-image, and alter her own life for the better. We summarise this analysis in Figure 5.2 on the next page.

By focusing on individual cases in our discussion of networks, we have sought to drive home a critical point that is overlooked in the structural-functional models of development that dominate current thinking: proactive individual members of networks play the central role in development. When networks function as structures that simply follow routines, they eventually fail as zones of proximal development. Proactive individuals must use existing structures, but it is the individuals who are the source of the new ideas and activities needed to adapt and change zones of proximal development. Zones of proximal development require constant revitalisation through innovative individuals if they are to remain adequate sources of knowledge for community members to draw on in solving everyday problems. Research on development should spend more effort in articulating the role of such individuals and the zones of proximal development.

Figure 5.2: Individual and community networking in the escape from poverty

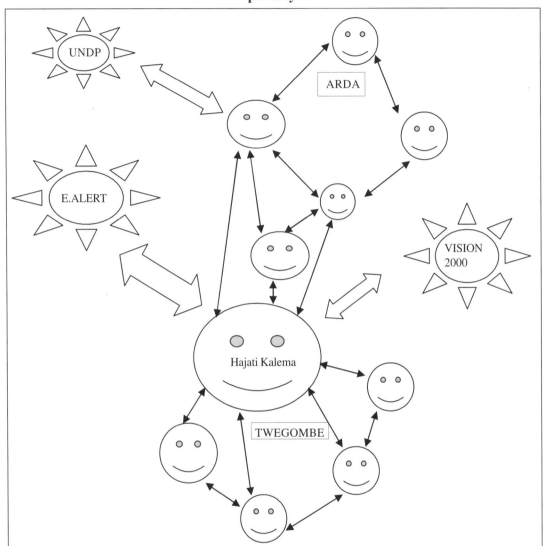

Conclusion

This chapter examined ways that interaction among individual peasants keeps them in poverty or helps them to escape it. Following Vygotsky (1978), we have focused on the specific processes that gave rise to the peasants' plight and to changes in it in order to understand their situation. Also in line with Vygotsky's view, we have seen how development began with cognitive re-orientation. Hajati Kalema set in motion a series of changes toward development by first correctly analysing the current state of the zone of proximal development in her adopted village and the critical knowledge that was lacking. She then set about providing knowledge herself, bringing others in to do so, and creating a community-based association that could generate and disseminate knowledge.

The success of this association derived in good measure from following known tenets of effective networks (Johnston and Lawrence, 1998; Knoke and Kuklinski, 1998, Willis, 1994). For instance, the agenda of the group derived from specific problems that members wanted to address; and members were free to join, leave, or even to discontinue the association. Through mobilising the support of an increasing number of members, the association achieved sufficient density of interaction to successfully institutionalise the value of crop farming and the methods of working with saline and rocky soils found in the communities.

We have applied the model of specific learning networks referred to as zones of proximal development to describe the processes through which the peasants moved out of poverty. This model describes individuals who first learn interpersonally, then internalise their learning, making it part of themselves through intrapersonal learning, and, finally, contribute creatively to the learning environment of others. The peasants from neighbouring villages who first learned from Twegombe and then set up their own association (ARDA) to cope with problems in their own community illustrated this process.

The formation of ARDA also illustrates Granovetter's (1973) argument that communities develop through the activities of individuals. This underlines the importance of balancing the usual focus on structures with a focus on individuals in order to help people escape from poverty. Following networking theory, this focus should be on the interactions among individuals in the role set. Studying such interaction yields insight into the specific zones of proximal development in the community where intervention is required. In answer to the question, "How did you join the project?", all respondents indicated that they did so through direct contact with other people, church, seminars and NGO officials. Several extracts from the interviews illustrate this networking:

> It was in 1994. I saw my friends rearing [silk]worms and I asked them about the project. They told me all it was about. I picked the interest and started rearing the cocoons with the intention of improving my standard of living.

> It was in 1992. A seminar was organised where I also attended and they started sensitising us about the project, how one can plant the mulberry, how one can rear the cocoons, and later get the cuttings of mulberry. And I started planting with an intention of earning a living.

> 1988, we had open wells, and people in the same areas came together and brought our problem to the RRD. Then the RRD told us to gather stones, clay, plus a well. Then the CBHC RRD inspected the place and gave cement and sent a technician of the springs and worked with him. He was paid by the CBHC under RRD.

These examples demonstrate the importance of networking for development. They reinforce the conclusion that without networking it is almost impossible to begin the process of escaping poverty.

The events described in this chapter also clarify the operation of structural holes (Burt, 1997) as a catalyst for development. That is, they show how the presence in a society of separate more or less independent associations that set their own agendas enables individuals to revitalise decaying zones of proximal development. Such associations were exemplified by UNDP, Environmental Alert, Twegombe, ARDA, and Vision 2000. Each association was an independent network that possessed its unique resources and its own agenda. Bridging individuals carried knowledge across the structural holes that separated these networks and thereby improved their own zones of proximal development.

The existence of multiple networks that are separated by structural holes provides their members with both the potential and the incentive to reach out and learn from other networks. The villagers who founded ARDA, for example, recognised that they had reached the boundaries of their capacity for growth because they heard about other associations that were doing better. These associations provided alternative zones of proximal development from which they could draw resources to revitalise their own atrophying zone. But for this to occur, there must be individuals who are willing and able to bridge the structural holes. This is not a simple matter, for such individuals must have special characteristics some of which were summarised by Frese (2000). We return to these characteristics in greater detail in Chapter 7.

---

1. Subsequent test of this theory has provided at least partial support for the relevance of weak ties (see Seibert, Kraimer, and Liden, 2001).

6

Participation and Development

The previous chapter examined the process of development from the viewpoint of the individual who is trying to escape poverty. We were especially concerned with the networks in which the individual is embedded and in how networking can be used to promote development, We distinguished individuals acting on their own from interacting with others and concluded that, although both are important, interacting is more critical for escaping from poverty. This chapter continues the debate by examining participation, a method central to the individual-in-development emphasis that we prefer. The ultimate aim of participatory development has been to take into account such human dimensions as values, motives, norms and solidarity. Ignoring such dimensions has contributed substantially to the failure of development initiatives (Uphoff, 2000).[1] The chapter is divided into two sections. The first section briefly discusses participation and distinguishes between system-maintaining and system-transforming participation. The second section draws upon the data collected in our empirical study to demonstrate the relevance of participation for escapting from poverty in selected projects.

Models of participatory development

In general terms 'participation' refers to people involving themselves indirectly or directly in organisations concerned with the decision-making about and implementation of development (Roodt, 1996, p.312). In practice, participation has been used to refer to implementation of project objectives, sharing in benefits, evaluation, and decision-making (Cohen & Uphoff, 1980).

The UNICEF (1986) report on participation in development describes seven different degrees of participation, namely: participation through the use of a service; contribution of resources; passive attendance at decision making meetings; consultation on particular issues; partnership involvement with other actors in delivering services; implementation of delegated powers; and involvement in decision-making at all levels (referred to in this chapter as managerial participation).

The objectives of participation include: empowerment, capacity building, goal attainment and cost sharing. The highest objective is empowerment, increasing participants' control over regulative institutions and resources. This objective is achieved when consumers and users initiate actions relevant to their own needs. The community then becomes owner-manager of the development project. A more limited objective is capacity building, enabling beneficiaries to take on management responsibilities such as routine decision-making in a project initiated from outside. A third, lower level objective is to increase the effectiveness of a project measured in terms of goal attainment. This objective is grounded in the assumption that beneficiary involvement fosters a better match between project services and beneficiary needs. The lowest level objective is cost sharing. This improves the efficiency of a project because involvement enhances collective understanding and agreement (Paul, 1990). These objectives of participation draw attention to a distinction between *system-maintaining* and *system-transforming* participation.

System-maintaining participation

This refers to participation through incorporation of people into projects rather than redistributing power to them. It leads to people-centred change based on the intervention of outsiders.The people-centred participatory approach to development grew out of traditional modernisation and dependency theories, which stressed economic growth and industrialisation. Modernisation and dependency theories of growth had at their base a concern with systems and procedures rather than with people. From the point of view of these theories, underdevelopment in third world countries was a problem of the affected people which the experts had to solve. The rural poor were seen as obstacles rather than as assets in furthering the process of development.

Projects and programmes to smooth the path of national development were designed, formulated, and implemented by urban planners and administrators without recourse to the rural populations who they regarded as traditional and primitive. These projects were imposed in a top down fashion with little consultation with the local people. Emphases were laid on providing the infrastructural facilities and institutions to facilitate changes. These strategies ignored the growing cleavages that the benefits of modernisation seemed to produce in societies and the growing disillusionment with the example of developed societies with their increasing social polarisation and unemployment problems (Sandbrook, 1982).

System-transforming participation

The above climate led to an increasing awareness that economic growth *per se* is not development. There must be more appropriate ways of developing a country, ways that do not destroy the ecology upon which all the people of the world ultimately depend (Korten, 1996). From this, the system-transforming, people-generated participatory approach to development was born. People-generated change depends on initiative-taking by beneficiaries themselves. People-generated change that aims at transforming the system is the kind of participation most likely to promote development. The participatory approach to development is a three pronged process. It entails a process of social investigation with the full and active participation of the community, an educational process of mobilisation for development, and a means of taking action for development (cited in Van Vlaenderen & Nkwinti, 1993, p.381).

One of the earliest advocats of system transforming participation was Vygotsky (1978), in his cultural theory of development. He averred that neither learning nor development takes place without participation. Rather, knowledge is constructed through interaction with others. People engage in activities such as learning how to crop farm on saline soil and come to a clear situational definition of their problems and available remedies. Working in collaboration with others provides the opportunity for people to reveal their capabilities (Gilbert, 1989) and also to acquire new knowledge from others. In this interaction, participants are able to go beyond their initial level of understanding of their surroundings and to analyse their social situation with critical awareness. As discussed and demonstrated in the last chapter, when this interaction is successful, it creates a new zone of proximal development or revitalises a previously atrophying one. When this happens, development takes place.

Participation in development projects and development

In this section, we briefly present and discuss factors and performance indicators that are associated with individual participation and moving out of poverty in development projects we visited. We examine variation in the nature of the participation of individuals in development projects. For example, are individuals in some projects more actively involved in initiating and managing projects than other individuals in other projects? Are there differences in attitudes toward active involvement and management? Are there gender differences in the nature of participation and attitudes? Are these differences related to the impact of projects on the lives of people who took part in the projects?

The measurement of development

In order to estimate whether the sample that participated in the various development projects changed their lives for the better as a result of participation, we need to specify indicators of benefit. The models discussed above and more recent empirical findings from studies of micro-finance institutions in Uganda guide us. Growth-centred models of participation suggest that indicators of project/business expansion are appropriate. In contrast, people-centred models suggest employing indicators of a decent human existence (justice), sustainability and inclusiveness (Sen, 1997, Snyder, 2000). In the following analysis we emphasise people-centred indicators but also use growth measures.

Two recent local studies by Snyder (2000) and Namatovu (2001), reported in Chapter 1, influenced our choice of what indicators to emphasise. In the terms we have adopted from Vygotsky, these studies concerned revitalising or expanding the zone of proximal development in communities. The development that occurred focused on how individuals gained capabilities rather than on gaining wealth or utility (see Alkire, 2001 for an operationalisation of this work). As in these studies, we anticipated that development among the poor people who constituted our study sample would largely take the form of learning to live more effectively rather than acquiring commodities including expanding their business. Development would refer to interpersonal and intrapersonal learning. We therefore decided to use indicators of qualitative development and change that would enable us to compare those who had gained capabilities as a result of participation and those who had not (see also Sen, 1997).

To elicit subjective information on individuals' development, we asked two questions both of participants and non-participants. First, we asked respondents whether their participation or their non-participation had affected their status in the community. Second, we asked each respondent to compare herself with her peers who had or had not

Table 6.1: Whether membership or non-membership has affected status in the community

Status outcome		Members	Non-members	Total
Lowered status	Count	1	50	51
	Row %	1.9	98.1	100
	Column %	0.35	58.8	13.8
	% of Total	0.3	13.5	13.7
No change	Count	30	29	59
	Row %	50.8	49	100
	Column %	10.5	34.1	15.9
	% of Total	8.1	7.8	15.9
Improved status	Count	194	5	199
	Row %	97.5	2.5	100
	Column %	68.1	5.9	53.8
	% of Total	52.4	1.8	54.2
Improved a lot	Count	60	1	61
	Row %	98.4	1.6	100
	Column %	21.1	1.2	16.5
	% of Total	16.2	0.27	16.47
Total	Count	285	85	370
	Row %	77.1	22.9	100
	Column %	100	100	100
	% of Total	77.1	22.9	100

Chi sq. = 243 df=3 $p < 0.001$

participated in the project. The following two tables show that participants gained more than non-participants. Table 6.1 indicates clearly that respondents who participated in a project thought that their participation was associated with an increased in their status. The vast majority of non-participants, on the other hand, thought that their status was unchanged or even lowered.

The data on relative status in response to the question on comparison of self to others support the same conclusion. The self-reported comparison in Table 6.2 confirms that people who took part in the projects saw themselves as gaining in status in comparison with those who did not. Conversely, those who did not participate perceived themselves as losing status compared to those who did.

Were there any gender differences in status perception as a result of taking part in development projects? Table 6.3 indicates that the perceived effects on one's status of participation in a project were not associated with gender. The column percentages indicate that 69 % of men and 68% of women perceived improved status. Another 20% of men and 21% of women perceived that their status had improved a lot.

On the question of whether participants perceived their status as higher or lower

Table 6. 2: Comparing status perceptions of non-members with members

Perceptions		Sample		
		Members	**Non-members**	**Total**
Lower than most	Count	4	55	59
	Row %	6.7	93	100
	Column%	1.4	70.5	16.3
	% of Total	1	15	16
Same as most	Count	18	15	33
	Row %	54.5	45.5	100
	Column %	6.3	19.2	9.1
	% of Total	4.9	4.1	9
Higher than most	Count	174	8	182
	Row %	95	5	100
	Column %	61.3	10.3	50.3
	% of Total	48	2	50
Much higher	Count	88		88
	Row %	100		100
	Column %	31		24.3
	% of Total	24		24
Total	Count	284	78	362
	Row %	78	21.5	100
	Column %	100	100	100
	% of Total	78	21.5	100

Chi sq. = 246 df=3 p < .000

than non-participants (Table 6.4) there was a small gender difference ($p<.05$). Approximately 10% of women as against 2% of men thought that their status was the same as or lower than those who had not participated. Among both men and women, however, the overwhelming majority thought that their status was higher or much higher than people who had not participated in the projects (97% of men, 89% of women). Throughout this study, we have recorded virtually no sex differences. We therefore question the reliability of this small difference.

In sum, approximately 90% of participants perceived improvement in their status both absolutely and in comparison to non-participants. We introduced some of the reasons for this in the last chapter and explore why this should be so in greater detail in the next chapter. To anticipate that discussion, we found that participants learned how to solve problems that everyone around knew they could not solve before they joined. Moreover, the problems the participants learned to solve were also community-wide problems that all members of the community would have wanted to be able to solve as well. Next, we look indirectly at some of these problems by examining the motives participants reported for joining development projects.

Table 6.3: Whether participation has promoted status of respondnet:
Gender differences

Perceived status		Gender		Total
		Men	**Women**	
Lowered status	Count	1		1
	Row %	100		100
	Column %	1		0.4
	% of Total	0.4		0.4
No change	Count	8	21	29
	Row %	27	72	100
	Column %	9	11	10
	% of Total	2.8	7	10
Improved status	Count	61	132	193
	Row %	31.6	68	100
	Column %	69	68	68
	% of Total	21.6	46.8	68
Improved status a lot	Count	18	41	59
	Row %	30.5	69	100
	Column %	20	21	20.9
	% of Total	6	14.5	20.9
Total	Count	88	194	282
	Row %	31	68.7	100
	Column %	100	100	100
	% of Total	31	68.7	100

Chi Sq. = 2.4   df= 3   p=.4

Motivation for joining projects

In order to assess motivation to join projects, we asked participants: Now I would like to hear about the reasons why you became part of this project. That is, why did you join it? After hearing the participants' spontaneous reasons, the interviewer asked the participants to rate the importance of each of the reasons listed in Table 6.5 as a reason to join the project, using a 1 to 4 scale of importance. We factor analysed responses using orthogonal rotation. Three factors emerged. Table 6.5 gives item loadings greater than 0.35 on these factors.

We labelled the motive factor that accounts for the largest proportion of variance in participants' responses (32%) 'mastering one's environment'. The items that compose this motive (1–5) capture the people-generated type of participation discussed above. Item 1 refers to participants joining a project in order to get what they need in life. Items 2-5 identify what it is that respondents needed or lacked. We had constructed these items based on respondents' replies to the open-ended question that asked the respondents to tell us why they joined the projects. The clustering of these items on the first factor indicate that what the respondents needed out of life was to obtain better food and water, learn new skills, increase income, and get help with marketing.

Table 6.4: Perceived influence of participation on community status: Gender effects

Perceived comparison		Gender		Total
		Men	Women	
Lower than most	Count	1	3	4
	Row %	25	75	100
	Column %	1	1.5	1.4
	% of Total	0.3	1	1.4
Same as most	Count	1	17	18
	Row %	5.5	94	100
	Column %	1	8.8	6.4
	% of Total	0.3	6	6
Higher than most	Count	63	109	172
	Row %	36.6	63.4	100
	Column %	71.5	56.5	61
	% of Total	22.4	38.7	61
Much higher than most	Count	23	64	87
	Row %	26.4	73.6	100
	Column %	26	33	30.9
	% of Total	8	22.7	30.9
Total	Count	88	193	281
	Row %	31	68.6	100
	Column %	100	100	100
	% of Total	31	68.6	100

Chi Sq.= 8.8 df= 3 p <.05

Interestingly, although all the respondents were engaged in income generating activities, none mentioned becoming a successful entrepreneur and getting richer as a reason for joining projects. Rather, they focused on learning how to master their environment through learning new ways of living such as how to obtain better food and water and how to market their produce. The last chapter used network analysis to demonstrate how participants learned to master their environment and to escape from poverty by interacting with others rather than by acting on their own.

We labelled the second motive factor 'altruism or concern for others' (items 6, 7, and 8). Those for whom this type of motive was important were concerned with doing what is expected of them, as item 6 indicates. In the Ugandan society, this often means helping your neighbour whenever you can. So, overall, this factor referred to actions that would benefit others, partially motivated by conformity.

We labelled the third motive factor 'helping family and self.' Items 9 and 10 referred to helping their family through meeting its needs and specifically raising its standard of living. It is probably that respondents understood item 11 as referring to formal education rather than to practical skills. For this reason, it did not fall on the first factor that concerned mastering the environment

Table 6.5: Factor analysis of motives for joining projects

Motives	Mastering one's environment	Altruism/ concern for others	Helping family and self
1 .Gain what I need or lack in my daily life by participating	0.88		
2. Obtain better/ more food & water	0.88		
3. Learn new skills	0.88		
4. Increase my income, obtain more money	0.82		
5. Get help with market- what I want to sell or trade	0.62		
6. Avoid acting against what others (e.g. spouse, family) wanted me to do		0.78	
7. Serve my church (people of my religion)		0.70	
8. Help the needy and my society		0.62	
9. Provide better for the needs of my family			0.76
10. Improve my standard of living			0.65
11. Obtain new knowledge and experience			-0.53
Eigen value	3.8	1.9	1.5
Percent of variance accounted for	32.0	16.0	13.0

When people join a project in order to master their environments and to acquire new competencies, they are more likely to sustain their commitments to the project over time, so the project objectives are more likely to be attained. Of course, this assumes that the zone of proximal development that the project establishes or revitalises does not atrophy. That is, it assumes that the project can continue to provide new opportunites to learn. If, on the other hand, people join to serve non-competence oriented motives or short-term motives such as simply making more money, the project is less likely to be sustained and meet its objectives.

We next examined whether there were regional differences in people's motives for joining projects. Table 6.6 shows that people from the Central region were significantly different on all the three motives. In the Central region, participants were more motivated to master their environment, to help others and to improve the standard of living of their

Table 6.6: Regional variations in the motives for joining projects

Motives	Regions	N	Mean	SD	df	F	Sig.
Joined project	Western	48	2.5	2.9	2,153	88	0
to master one's	Northern	49	4.6	3.7			
environment	Central	57	11.7	4.3			
	Total	154	6.5	5.4			
Joined project to	Western	48	2	1.9	2,287	3.6	0.03
help	Northern	50	1.9	2.8			
	Central	190	2.6	1.6			
	Total	288	2.4	1.9			
Joined project to	Western	48	4.7	2.3	2,287	41	0
improve standard	Northern	50	5.8	1.9			
of self and family	Central	190	7.1	1.4			
	Total	288	6.5	1.9			

Note: The differences in N in the regions is because some respondents did not answer some questions.

families. These differences are consistent with the national statistics which indicate that on the whole the Central region is economically better off than the other two regions we studied. The greater motivation in this region implies a higher level of social capital, a point we discuss in the next chapter.

Table 6.7 shows that men and women did not differ in the extent to which they were motivated to join projects in order to master the environment through acquiring skills, knowledge, and markets. However, the motive for joining projects in order to improve the standard of living of family and self and to help others was more important to women. This is consistent with recent findings that indicate that women who join micro-finance projects do so for the purpose of improving the welfare of their families rather than for profit through business entrepreneurship (Snyder, 2000; Namatovu, 2001).

Table 6.7: Gender differences in motives for participating

Motives	Gender	N	Mean	SD	t	df	Sign.
Joined project to	Male	62	5.9	5	-1.2	148	0.21
master one's	Female	88	7	5.7			
environment							
Joined project to help	Male	88	1.9	2.2	-2.7	282	0.01
Female		196	2.6	1.8			
			6				
Joined project to	Male	88	6	1.8	-2.7	282	0.01
improve standard	Female	196	6.7	1.9			
of self and family							

Table 6.8: Mean scores for involvement in and evaluation of initiating and managing projects as a function of district and region

Region	District	Involvement in initiation	Involvement in management	Evaluation of local management
Western	Bushenyi n=22	1.2 (6)	4.8 (2)	16.4 (5)
Kabale n=26	-	5 (1)		21 (1)
Northern	Arua n = 22	2.4 (2)	4.5 (3)	19 (2)
	Nebbi n=29	2.3 (3)	4.4 (4)	18.6 (3)
Central	Mukono n=71	2.5 (1)	2.5 (6)	16 (6)
	Masaka n=81	1.4 (5)	1.3 (7)	13 (7)
	Mpigi n=40	2.3 (3)	3.4 (5)	17.5 (4)
F		4.5	41.6	22
df		6,215	6,286	6,263
p<		.001	.001	.001

* Bracketed figures are ranks. There is no mean for Kabale under 'Involvement in initiation because none of the respondents from Kabale answered the relevant questions.

Regional and gender differences in the nature of participation in development projects

We next examined variation in the nature of participation in development projects across regions and individuals. Were individuals in some districts more actively involved in initiating and managing projects than those in other districts? Were there differences in attitudes toward active involvement and management? Were there gender differences in the nature of participation and attitudes?

In order to measure whether local people were involved in initiating actions in projects we summed 'yes' responses across four items: local people initiating project, initiating actions themselves, coming together on their own, being more responsible than outsiders for initiating actions. These items are questions 1, 3, 5, and 6 of the protocol. The alpha coefficient for the four item index was 0.73. In order to measure involvement in management we summed responses across the following five items: local people manage project, set project objectives, initiate actions, influence project running, and sustain the project financially (alpha coefficient = 0.84). Finally, we asked respondents to evaluate involvement of locals in managing projects. Repeating the five items referring to management of projects, we asked whether they thought local involvement in each of these was very bad (1), bad (2), neither or depends (3), good (4), or very good (5). The alpha coefficient for this index was 0.82.

Table 6.8 reports the mean responses in each district. Project participants in Mukono and Arua report the highest level of initiation of projects, while those in Masaka and Bushenyi were least involved in initiating projects. At the level of regions (West, North, Central) rather than districts, however, involvement in initiation did not differ (F= 1.6; df 2,219; p = 0.2). Involvement in management was greatest in Kabale, followed by Bushenyi, Arua, and Nebbi. Participants in Masaka and Mukono were the least involved. The difference between the regions on management is significant and in favour of

Western Uganda (F=80;df=2,290;p=0.000). Local involvement in management was greatest in the Western Uganda region and least in the Central region (F= 80; df 2,290; p < 0.001). Evaluation of local involvement in the management of projects varied significantly across districts. It was most positive in Kabale and least positive in Masaka. With the exception of Bushenyi, the districts where local management was highest also valued it most. This matching of actual involvement in management with a positive evaluation of management held across regions, with participants in Western and Northern Uganda evaluating local management more positively than in the Central region (F= 25.9; df 2,267; p < 0.001).

As noted several times previously, women experience more poverty than men in Uganda. We were therefore interested in whether there were gender differences in attitudes toward participation in the initiation and management of projects. Table 6.9 reveals differences between men and women on management but not on initiation. More men than women manage projects, reflecting the general trend for men more than women to occupy managerial positions. The third column shows, however, that women are less satisfied with local management. This may be an indication of their being left out of managerial functions, or it may be a genuine evaluation of the way local people (mainly men) run projects.

Table 6.9: Mean scores for involvement in and evaluation of project participation as a function of gender

Groups	Involvement in initiation	Involvement in management	Evaluation of local management
Males (66,91,76)	1.9	3.6	17.3
Females (153,198,191)	2.1	2.7	15.8
T	0.75	3.7	2.6
df	217	287	265
Significance	0.45	0.000	0.01

*Numbers of respondents (in brackets) varied across items due to missing data.

Problems encountered in projects

In order to identify the problems that respondents encountered with projects, we asked: What major problems, if any, has the project faced? Respondents received a list of 15 potential problems and were invited to add others. Table 6.10 indicates the proportion of project participants who reported encountering each problem.

The most frequently reported problem, mentioned by 41% of all project participants, was failure of other project members to meet their commitments. Other problems with fellow project participants were also common: non-attendance at meetings (25%) and lack of enthusiasm (19%). Difficult objective conditions, most prominently lack of funds (36%), but also lack of markets, land, water, and machinery, and problems with transportation were mentioned by a number of participants (13-20%). Thus, most projects are apparently not hindered by such problems, but they occur frequently enough

Table 6.10: Percentage of participants who reported encountering various problems in projects

Problem	Percent reporting problem (n=293)
Lack of enough land	14
Lack of sufficient funds	36
Lack of water	15
Lack of markets	20
Transportation	17
Non-attendance at meetings	26
Lack of trained personnel	11
Lack of transparency (corruption)	4
Lack of machinery/equipment	13
Opposition from local people	9
Opposition from government	2
Lack of enthusiasm	19
Failure to meet commitments	41
Methods learned don't work	0
Demands too much work	10
Discrimination	4

to merit attention. On the other hand, few participants complained of what they were learning from the project sponsors or how the projects were run; none mentioned that the methods did not work; very few accused the projects of corruption or discrimination; and only a few noted a lack of trained personnel. Moreover, both government and local people were seen as largely supportive of the projects.

There was a small but significant correlation between the total number of problems a participant reported and whether the project they were in was managed locally (r=. 22, p<0. 05). We speculate that this reflects the difficulties of accessing resources locally without outside help, which may also contribute to the problems of commitment. This is not necessarily a negative evaluation of local management, but a simple fact.

Given the high frequency of lack of commitment and failure to attend meetings, we examined possible reasons for low involvement in the projects. We asked: 'Here are some people or things that might prevent you from being more involved in the project. Do any of these prevent you from being more involved?' Table 6.11 reports the percentage of participants who agreed that their involvement was inhibited for various reasons.

The major reason given for low involvement was that the project did not serve personal interests. The low frequency of the other reasons for low involvement suggests that significant others rarely interfere with participants' involvement but that they commit themselves to the extent that the project is meaningful to them.

Table 6.11. Percentage of participants reporting that various sources prevented them from being more involved in projects

Reason	Percent reporting (n=240-293)
My parents prevent me	2%
My husband prevents me	9%
I have a lot of other work to do	2%
Activities are time consuming	9%
Activities do not serve my interests	36%
There is little benefit to me	8%

Case study 5.3 in Chapter 5 demonstrates this well. Hajati Kalema, the founder of Twegombe, tried to persuade an individual who she thought needed the kind of services and skills that Twegombe offered. This individual, who had a clear interest in being with other people, but not necessarily in the skills that Twegombe offered, resisted Hajati but instead joined another network, which focused on entertainment. It was only when this network failed that the individual in question finally joined Twegombe. The individual joined primarily to be with people and secondarily to learn new methods of agriculture and animal husbandry.

Success of performance in projects and its correlates

We consider here a number of different indicators of how well project participants succeeded in their project activity and some correlates of this success. Participants in almost all projects received either a monetary loan or a loan of materials. Hence, one indicator of successful project performance is repayment of loans by the due date. Although most loans (64%) did not charge interest, the vast majority (90%) had a set repayment date. For 60% of the project participants we interviewed, this date had already come, and 79% of these participants had succeeded in repaying their loan in time.

Another set of questions asked whether the project participant controlled the decisions she or he made about the way to run the project or whether decision-making was shared with or was in the hands of other household members. Because we are especially interested in whether men and women participate differently in the projects, we compared the responses of male and female project members. Table 6.12 reports the percentages of male and female respondents who indicated that they or others had decision-making control.

The responses indicate that whether the project participant is a woman or man it does not influence the degree of control he or she exercises over decisions related to the way the project is run. In most cases, the participant had full control, though spouses had some influence on the utilisation of assets. The much talked about lack of control women normally experience in projects of this nature was not in evidence here.

The importance of this finding lies in the objectives of projects for the poor, which normally target specific individuals or categories of individuals. If those who are targeted

Table 6.12:Percentages of respondents who exercise control over various decisions related to the project

Type of decision	Male project members	Female project members
How to use loans/or materials	81%	86%
What to do with savings from the project	84%	82%
How to utilise or dispose of assets such as land or equipment	59%	68%

for help are not able to exercise control, then the reasons for helping them have been ignored. The earlier literature we reviewed showed that one of the reasons for introducing these projects was to empower and to build capacity. Neither empowerment nor capacity building are likely if decision-making lies outside the control of the target beneficiary. Hence, control of these projects should be in the hands of the individuals for whom the projects were intended.

The preceding analyses indicate that project members made their own decisions regarding the project and were meeting at least the minimum requirement of paying back loans. We next examined whether the projects were growing and earning income for their participants. A series of questions asked about the contributions of the project to employment, goods for trading and sale, customer growth, and income. Again, we assessed whether there were gender differences in growth and earnings. Table 6.13 presents the percentages of respondents who agreed that the project contributed in various ways.

Most projects contributed regular income to participants, helped to expand business and increased the number of customers. There was also substantial employment of

Table 6.13: Percentages of men and women project members who reported that the project made each type of contribution

Type of contribution	Men (84)	Women (93)
Use family employees	23%	23%
Employ outsiders	66%	30%
Business expanding /having more to sell	67%	70%
Business expanding /having more customers	68%	67%
Regular income from project	77%	79%

Note: Numbers varied by question.

outsiders and some employment of family members. Men and women fared similarly with the exception of employing outsiders, where men employed larger numbers (t = 5.7; df, 257; p<0.01). Although the proportions of men and women who received some regular income from projects did not differ, men may have received somewhat more income with somewhat more regularity. We concluded this from an additional analysis. We measured the regularity of income on a three-point scale: (1) earning a daily income that enabled living almost entirely on the proceeds of the project, (2) earning seasonally only as with crop farmers or small scale poultry farmers,[2] and (3) receiving an irregular income, as with earners who do not put enough effort into a particular business to predict when they are able to earn, investing in their business only when they have slack resources.

Table 6.14 indicates that only 6.6% of respondents (12.9% of men and 3.8% of women) rely on the daily income from a project for their survival. On the other hand, 74% of the participants earn irregularly from projects (64.3% men and 78% women). Men and women differ less in the percent relying on projects for seasonal earnings. Overall, men obtain more regular earnings from the projects than women (Chi Sq. 7.7; df 2; p < 0.05). From the table we learn that few project members rely completely on their projects for daily survival. This does not necessrily indicate that the projects were inappropriate or unsuccessful. Most people had joined the project within the year or two preceding our interview with them. Most small businesses begin to break even

Table 6.14: Regularity with which project participants earn income from the project by gender

Regularity of contribution		Sex		Total
		Male	Female	
Daily	Count	9	6	15
	Row %	60	40	100
	Column %	12.9	3.8	6.6
	% of Total	3.98	2.7	6.6
Seasonal	Count	16	28	44
	Row %	36.4	64	100
	Column %	22.9	18	19
	% of Total	7.08	12	19
Irregular	Count	45	122	167
	Row %	26.9	73	100
	Column %	64.3	78	74
	% of Total	19.9	54	74
Total	Count	70	156	226
	Row %	31	69	100
	Column %	100	100	100
	% of Total	31	69	100

Table 6.15: Regularity with which project participants earn income from the project by region and district

Region			How regular			Total
			Daily	Seasonal	Irregular	
Western	Bushenyi	Count	5	5	1	11
		Row %	45	45	9.1	100
		Column %	33	11	0.6	4.8
		Total %	2.2	2.2	0.4	4.8
	Kabale	Count	4	5	2	11
		Row %		36	45	18	100
		Column %	27	11	1.2	4.8
		Total %	1.7	2.2	0.9	4.8
Northern	Arua	Count	1	11	8	20
		Row %	5	55	40	100
		Column %	6.7	24	4.7	8.7
		Total %	0.4	4.8	3.5	8.7
	Nebbi	Count	1	8	17	26
		Row %	3.8	31	65	100
		Column %	6.7	18	10	11
		Total %	0.4	3.5	7.4	11
Central	Mukono	Count	3	3	66	72
		Row %	4.2	4.2	92	100
		Column %	20	6.7	39	31
		Total %	1.3	1.3	29	31
	Masaka	Count		4	48	52
		Row %		7.7	92	100
		Column %		8.9	28	23
		Total %		1.7	21	23
	Mpigi	Count	1	9	27	37
		Row %	2.7	24	73	100
		Column %	6.7	20	16	16
		Total %	0.4	3.9	12	16
Total		Count	15	45	169	229
		Row %	6.6	20	74	100
		Column %	100	100	100	100
		Total %	6.6	20	74	100

Table 6.16: Economic activities that project participants from each district engage in

District	Total (n)	Catering industry	Distribu-tive trade	Live-stock farming	Repairs	Crop farm-ing	Produc-tion	Other service
West								
Bushenyi	24	0%	4.2%	4.2%	0%	25%	54.1%	12.5%
Kabale	24	0%	0 %	12.6%	0%	8.3%	70.8%	8.3%
North								
Arua	22	0%	22.7%	0%	18.2%	18.2%	31.8%	9.1%
Nebbi	29	13.5%	20.7%	10.3%	3.5%	13.8%	27.6%	20.6%
Central								
Mpigi	39	0%	0%	30.8%	0%	69.2%	0%	0%
Mukono	75	16%	30.7%	14.7%	14.7%	6.7%	6.7%	10.5%
Masaka	80	5%	28.8%	26.3%	3.8%	26.3%	2.2%	7.6%

after the fifth year. Hence, the youthfulness of the projects might well explain the low percentages of people for whom they could provide sufficient daily resources.

We also investigated the extent to which projects in different regions of Uganda provided regular income to their participants. The results, in Table 6.15, demonstrate substantial regional differences. In all of the districts of the Central region, most projects provided little daily income (ranging from 0% in Masaka to 20% in Mukono). Participants from Bushenyi (33%) and Kabale (27%) took the lead in relying on their projects for daily income. Masaka has the highest number of people who earn only irregularly from their projects (92%). The data from this table should be interpreted with care, however, because many people did not answer this question. The question was probably confusing because very few people in Uganda earn from a single source. The environment has never been stable enough for Ugandans to specialise in this manner. With hindsight, we recognise that the question posed here was problematic.

Table 6.16 reports the percentage of respondents who engage in various money-earning activites. Most of these activities are not capable of providing enough income for daily survival.

Examination of Table 6.16 reveals why the income earned from projects in the Central region is especially irregular. Project participants from this region are engaged more in activities that are seasonal and cannot provide income on a daily basis. For example, 100% of those from Mpigi are engaged in livestock and crop farming. This compares with 52% in Masaka, 21% in Mukono, 21% in Nebbi, 18% in Arua, 29% in Bushenyi, and 20% in Kabale.

In order to assess the extent to which participants relied on income from different sources, including the projects, for normal expenditures, we took a two step approach. First, we asked them about the nature of their expenditures, for instance, for their

Table 6.17: Factors and loadings >.5 on sources of income

Major source of income when meeting specific needs	Components of income source				
	1	**2**	**3**	**4**	**5**
	Spouse	Project proceeds	Other businesses	Wage or paid employment	Relatives
Spouse footed educational bills	0.88				
Spouse was most important source of income in the last 12 months	0.81				
Spouse footed medical bills	0.81				
Spouse footed food bills	0.79				
Project proceeds footed the medical bills		0.79			
Project proceeds footed the food bills		0.74			
Project was most important source of income in the last 12 months		0.71 0.71			
Project proceeds footed educational bills		0.7			
My other businesses footed the medical bills			0.89		
My other businesses footed the food bills		0.78			
My other businesses footed the educational bills		0.76			
Selling my own labour footed educational bills				0.77	
Respondents' salary most important source of income in the last 12 months				0.75	
Relatives footed educational bills					0.85
Relatives helped with medical bills					0.78
Eigen Value	2.9	2.2	2.1	1.5	1.4
% of Variance	19	14.9	13.9	10.2	9.4
Cumulative %	19	34	48.3	58	67.8

Table 6.18: Mean reliance on varied sources of income by district

Region	District	Relying on spouse	Relying on project	Relying on other business	Relying on relative	Relying on wages/ salaries
Western (n=24)	Bushenyi	.12 (7)	2.4 (4)	1.5 (1)	0 (4)	.75 (1)
(n=24)	Kabale	1.3 (2)	2 (7)	1.2 (5)	0 (4)	.5 (2)
Northern (n=22)	Arua	.18 (5)	2.1 (6)	1.4 (3)	.22 (1)	.5 (2)
(n=29)	Nebbi	.13 (6)	2.4 (4)	1.4 (3)	.13 (2)	.27 (4)
Central (n=75)	Mukono	1.4 (1)	3.4 (1)	.9 (7)	0 (4)	0 (6)
(n=80)	Masaka	.73 (4)	3.1 (2)	1.5 (1)	.1 (3)	.13 (5)
(n=39)	Mpigi	1.3 (2)	2.9 (3)	1 (6)	0 (4)	0 (6)
	F	7.7	8	2.1	2.7	10
	df	6,286	6,286	6,286	6,286	6,286
p<		.001	.001	.05	.01	.001

Note: * Numbers in brackets are ranks.

childrens' schooling, for treatment when sick, for medical bills, and for domestic expenses including food. We also asked them what sources they drew on for these expenditures and a general question on the most important source of income in the last 12 months. The respondents chose from several options: spouse, project, salary, other businesses, relatives, and selling one's labour. We factor analysed these answers using varimax rotation and identified five interpretable factors that fit the options provided. (See Table 6.17, p.120.) (The instrument had questions that were brought together to enable the running of a factor analysis.)

Based on these factors, we created factor scores for each source of income and examined the importance of the project relative to other sources of income in the different districts. Table 6.18 reveals that reliance on spouses was least in Bushenyi and Arua followed by Masaka. Further analysis indicated that the low reliance on spouses in Bushenyi was due to the fact that its sample was predominantly male. In general, women relied significantly more on their spouses than men did ($t = 7$; df 287; p< 0.001).

Reliance on their projects for income was greatest in the Central region. The leading district here is Mukono, followed by Masaka and Mpigi. The projects in the Central region can therefore be considered to have had a greater impact on the lives of individual

Table 6.19: Means showing major sources of income by sex

Sources of earning	Sex	N	Mean	t	df	p<
Those relying on partner's income	Male	91	0.1	7	87	0.001
	Female	198	1.2			
Those relying on their project	Male	91	2.8	0.6	287	0.5
	Female	198	2.9			
Those relying on other sources	Male	91	1.4	1.2	287	0.2
	Female	198	1.2			
Get from relative	Male	91	0.1	0.4	287	0.6
	Female	198	0.1			
Paid employment	Male	91	0.3	2	287	0.04
	Female	198	0.2			

Table 6.20: Correlations of motives for joining projects with sources of income

Source of income	Joined project to master the environment	Joined project to help others	Joined project to improve standard of living
spouse/partner	0.07	0.06	0.13*
project	0.32**	0.06	0.12*
other sources	-0.07	0.08	-0.1
relatives	-0.10	0.06	-0.01
paid employment	-0.31**	0.01	-0.19**

participants. This finding is consistent with the greater social capital found in this region as compared to the others (see Chapter 7). Reliance on extra businesses for income was greatest in Masaka in Central and Bushenyi in the West regions, followed by Arua and Nebbi in the North. Participants in the North relied most on relatives as compared to other regions. Wage earning was most important in the West where Bushenyi ranked first, followed by Kabale and the two Northern districts. The samples from the Central region relied least on wage earning. This is consistent with their greater reliance on project proceeds.

We also examined gender differences in sources of income. As already indicated, women relied more on their spouses than men did. Table 6.19 shows a significant difference (p<0.001). On the other hand, men relied more on paid employment than women (p<0.04). Men and women did not differ in their reliance on the other sources of income–the project, other businesses, and relatives.

Finally, we asked whether the main sources of income on which participants relied were related to the reasons why they joined projects. Table 6.20 (above) provides the correlations between sources of income and motives for joining the project. Deriving one's primary income from the project correlated positively with having joined in order to master one's environment, that is, to acquire skills, knowledge and help with the marketing of produce and getting better food. The causal relationship underlying this correlation is probably reciprocal. People who were more strongly motivated to learn by joining a project may well have applied themselves more and hence succeeded more in generating income. On the other hand, quality projects that promised greater opportunities to learn may have attracted people who were motivated to learn. Consistent with the latter causal process, the motivation to improve one's standard of living also correlated positively with relying on one's project for income.

The positive correlation between relying on one's partner and joining the project to improve one's standard of living is revealing. Recall that this source of income was chosen almost exclusively by women. Women, in particular, apparently joined projects to increase their independence of their partners. For example, one woman said that now that she had joined a project she no longer had to ask for school fees for her children from the husband. Above, we treated relying on one's partner for income, even when one is a project participant, as a possible sign of lack of success of the project. It may well be, however, that women who have participated in a project only for a couple of years are moving toward independence but that the project has not yet matured enough to relieve their dependence on their partner. What is clear is that more than a few women join projects in order to reduce dependency on a spouse.

Deriving one's primary income from paid employment correlated negatively with joining projects to master the environment or to improve one's standard of living. This correlation indicates that those who rely on their jobs join projects for motives that have little to do with generating income for self and family. It is consistent with our speculation that the Northern region sample, with the top-down Northern Reconstruction Programme, joined projects because they had been brought to them. This is distinct from the Central region where individuals sought out such projects. This interpretation is reinforced by the data in Table 6.18 that indicate that respondents in the North and West relied most on wage employment rather than projects. Another possibility is that those who were engaged in paid employment tended more to see the projects more as sidelines rather than as significant supplementary sources of future income.

Conclusion

This chapter has examined some characteristics of projects and of participants and relations between them. We have looked at whether it was profitable or not for people to join projects. We made the assumption that those whose major source of income is the project are the ones who have succeeded more in their project. We found that the reliance on the projects as a primary source of income was greatest in the Central region and least in the Northern region. Using such indicators of success as people's self-reports that the methods they had been taught were working and that they had been able to repay the loans they had received when joining the projects, we concluded that the projects were succeeding, at least in the Central region.

On the larger questions about relations of participation to development, our findings lend further support to the growing evidence that development, as distinct from growth, is about acquiring a series of competencies, 'learnings', or capabilities that allow the individual to master his or her environment. Projects assist in doing this by creating a zone of proximal development where individuals can learn through interaction with others, to internalise this learning, and to use the internalised learning in solving subsequent problems. Our findings show that the motive for joining projects of 'mastering the environment' was stronger in the Central region, the region considered better off economically than the others. There was also more reliance on project income for solving daily economic problems in this region than in either of the others.

This chapter examined whether the structure of participation or the motives of individuals had a greater impact on the success of projects. We measured the structure of participation in terms of involvement in management and initiation of projects and evaluation of such involvement. From the reasons respondents gave for joining a project we derived three major motives: mastering the environment through acquiring capacities, improving one's standard of living, and helping people. We used the degree of reliance on project proceeds for daily living as the measure of project success. The analyses indicated that the structure of participation had little relationship to project success. However, motives for joining, particularly the motive of mastering the environment, correlated significantly with project success. This might indicate that participation is important in development but only so long as the motives of participants are congruent with the objectives of the project. The structure of projects may be important. However, it appears that the reasons that poor individuals join projects play a larger part in their success than the nature of their participation.

Our findings are consistent with the view that system-transforming participation is a continuous learning process that involves acquisition of knowledge and skills to help individuals solve their problems. Individuals acquire knowledge through engagement with others in authentic activity. Adults can see themselves as 'doers' who have the potential to mold their lives in ways they want and to fight hard for recognition of their ability to regulate their own lives (cf. Knowles, 1970). As discussed in earlier chapters, individual differences in self-conceptions, goals and personal values explain why some people decide to join projects while others choose not to do so.

Our findings are consistent with the view that system-transforming participation is a continuous learning process that involves acquisition of knowledge and skills to help individuals solve their problems. Individuals acquire knowledge through engagement with others in authentic activity. They can see themselves as 'doers' who have the potential to mold their lives in ways they want and to fight hard for recognition of their ability to regulate their own lives (cf. Knowles, 1970). As discussed in earlier chapters, individual differences in self-conceptions, goals and personal values explain why some people decide to join projects while others choose not to do so.

Central to the active involvement in development is individual self-regulation. This refers to the systematic orientation of one's self-generated thoughts, feelings and actions toward attainment of one's goals (Henderson & Cunningham, 1994). From the perspective of Vygotsky, self-regulation concerns the co-ordination of several human mental processes like memory, analysis, evaluation, planning, and creating a psychological system within the context of evaluation. Individuals construct knowledge they can use in goal attainment within a social context in which the ideas and actions of others affect them. Our research reveals how the respondents engaged in self-regulation, employing the full set of mental processes in social context. Through contact with family and community members and with outsiders involved in projects (African and European), individuals formulated goals, generated reasons for joining and acquired skills and knowledge. The processes that lead to development entailed system transformation. Projects contribute to development to the extent that they help individuals to identify problems, facilitate learning through individual participation and utilisation of skills.

1. The literature on participation and development is accumulating in two parallel forms. The first deals with theories of participatory development. The second focuses on the methodology of participation. This chapter deals with the theories rather than the methods.
2. Small-scale poultry farmers target their raising of broilers and trying to sell them to particular seasons such as Christmas or Easter.

7
Escaping Poverty:
The Relevance of Social Capital

The action view of culture we have adopted in this work allows us to see culture as the context within which new ideas such as the market economy must be negotiated (Diagne & Ossebi, 1996). We also noted that this action view has found support in the idea of social capital and certain theories of cultural and individual level values. This chapter examines social capital as a vehicle for escaping poverty. In keeping with our general analytic model, we present both quantitative and qualitative data. We use a limited set of quantitative data for two purposes. First we quantify the levels of social capital that characterise our samples. Second, we link our concept of value-based social capital to some of the measures of performance discussed in Chapters 4 and 6. The main part of the chapter presents qualitative analyses in order to examine the processes of becoming poor or of escaping poverty and to illustrate the relevance of social capital to these processes.

Chapter 3 discussed social capital as a cultural interface at length. There we described it as the meeting of complementary institutions. We briefly recall some central points of our argument to provide the underpinnings of the analyses that follow.

More elaborately, we conceptualised social capital as the sharing by members of a community of a set of cognitions (beliefs, values, attitudes, expectations and knowledge) which they intentionally sustain through structures such as roles, rules, and networks. These shared cognitions motivate communities and their members to protect, maintain, and enhance their relationships. They enable people to reach similar judgements and evaluations of what outcomes are desirable and undesirable and what behaviour is rational or not. This promotes the assumption that others are trustworthy and leads individuals to believe they can draw on others for cooperative action when necessary. These shared cognitions can motivate community members to cooperate in joint pursuits and enable them better to predict one another's behaviour.

With this brief reminder, we are ready to present a set of propositions that articulate the relationship between social capital and development.

Propositions

Based on the literature on social capital (particularly, Putnam et al., 1993; Coleman, 1988; Widner, 1998; Uphoff, 2000), we propose that the level of social capital in a community is greater to the extent that the following nine conditions are present. Members of the community:

1. Share similar cognitions and develop supporting structures for them.
2. Are able to trust each other and to perform acts of reciprocity.
3. Perform premeditated volunteerism aimed at serving their individual interests by enabling the community.

4.   Trust each other enough to engage regularly in wide ranging conversations.
5.   Are able to form and to belong to a variety of associations.
6.   Expect to be treated and are treated as equals within the community.
7.   Feel optimistic enough about their community to want to invest in it.
8.   Have information they are willing to share and which is useful in invigorating their community or zone of proximal development.
9.   Are able to link their community to the outside world.

These propositions were implied in Figures 3.1 and especially 3.2 in Chapter 3.

Quantitative assessment of social capital in the regions

Methods

In order to carry out quantitative analysis of social capital in our sample we built indexes from the data. First, we built indexes of two types of social capital, value-based bonding and bridging. Responses to items in the Portrait Values Questionnaire served to estimate variation among the different regions and individuals in the sample in cognitions that indicate social capital. We then correlated these indexes of social capital with two other indexes on which the regions differ, namely motives for joining projects (Table 6.7) and sources of income (Table 6.18).

As discussed in Chapter 3, the value items appropriate for representing value-based bonding social capital are those presumed to measure cultural embeddedness and egalitarianism, because they emphasise closeness within a community grounded in trust and reciprocity. The embeddeded community strives for and rewards a tranquil order, trust and willingness to reciprocate. On the other hand the egalitarian community encourages sharing and equality for all. The index of value-based bonding consisted of the following items (Table 7.1):

Table 7.1: Value-based bonding social capital

Embeddedness items in the Portrait Values Questionnaire

1. It is important to him/her to be polite to others all the time. He/She believes he/she should show respect to his/her parents and to older people

2. The safety of his/her country is very important to him/her. He/She wants his country to be safe from its enemies.

3. He/She thinks it is important not to ask for more than what you have. He/She believes that people should be satisfied with what they have.

4. It is important to him/her that everything is clean and in order. He/She really does not want things to be in a mess.

5. He/She believes that people should do what they are told. He/She thinks people should follow rules at all times even when no one is watching.

6. His/Her family's safety is extremely important to him/her. He/She would do anything to make sure his/her family is always safe.

7. It is important to him/her to fit in and do things the way other people do. He/She thinks he/she should do what others expect of him/her.

8. He/She thinks it is important to do things the way he/she learned from his/her family. He/She wants to follow their customs and traditions.

Table 7.1: Value-based bonding social capital (continued)

Egalitarianism items in the Portrait Values Questionnaire

1. He/She always wants to help the people who are close to him/her. It is very important to him/her to care for the people he/she knows and likes.

2. Honesty is very important to him/her. He/She believes he/she must be honest in any situation and always tell the truth.

3. It is important to him/her that his friends can always trust him/her. He/She wants to be loyal to them and always to look out for their interests.

4. He/She thinks it is important that every person in the world should be treated equally. He/She wants justice for everybody even for people he/she does not know.

As discussed in Chapter 3, the value items appropriate for representing value-based bridging social capital are those presumed to measure cultural mastery and intellectual autonomy. We defined bridging as the activity of linking identifiable actors such as networks, communities and individuals to other actors. Through bridging activities, groups and communities obtain skills, information, and other resources they need to overcome their own shortages of resources, shortages that prevent them from developing and progressing in the directions they desire (Temkin & Rohe, 1998). Bridging activities entail innovation, autonomy, and self-assertion to master problems in the environment. A community culture characterised by intellectual autonomy and mastery values encourages and legitimises bridging activities. The index of value-based bridging social capital consisted of the following items (Table 7.2):

Table 7.2: Value-based bridging social capital

Mastery items in the Portrait Values Questionnaire

1. Being very successful is important to him/her. He/She likes to stand out and to impress other people

2. He/She likes to make his/her own decisions about what he/she does. It is important to him/her to be free to plan and to choose activities for him/herself.

3. He/She likes people to know that he/she can do well. He/she is ambitious and ready to work hard and get ahead.

4. It is very important to him/her to show his/her abilities. He/She wants people to admire what he/she does.

Intellectual autonomy items in the Portrait Values Questionnaire

1. Thinking up new ideas and being creative is important to him/her. He/She likes to do things in his/her original way

2. It is important to him/her to listen to people who are different from him/her. Even when he/she disagrees with them, he/she still wants to understand them and to get along with them.

3. He/She thinks it is important to get interested in things. He/She is curious and tries to understand everything.

Table 7.3 (a): Comparing value-based social capital in the three regions (ANOVA)

Value-based social capital indices	Ugandan regions	N	Mean	Std. Dev.	df	F	Significance
Value-based bonding social capital	Western	40	4.3	0.5	2	109	001
	Northern	41	3.9	0.4			
	Central	183	4.9	0.4			
	Total	264	4.6	0.5			
Value-based bridging social capital	Western	43	4.5	0.5	2	21	.001
	Northern	49	3.8	0.6			
	Central	182	4.5	0.7			
	Total	274	4.4	0.7			
Combined bonding and bridging social capital	Western	38	8.9	85	2	65	.001
	Northern	41	7.7	.81			
	Central	178	9.5	.97			
	Total	257	9.1	1.1			

In addition to examining value-based bonding and bridging social capital separately, we combined them to form a single social capital index. Table 7.3 (a) presents results of an analysis that compared the levels of bonding and bridging social capital, and their combination across the three regions of Uganda. It reveals a significant difference between the regions on both value-based bonding and bridging social capital. Bonding social capital was highest in the Central region, followed by the Western and then the Northern region. Bridging social capital was equally high in the Central and Western regions and significantly lower in the Northern region.

To test the significance of the differences between all pairs of regions, we conducted post-hoc comparisons. Table 7.3 (b) on the following page presents the results. It shows that the Central region is significantly higher on bonding than the West and North regions, and significantly higher than the North region on bridging. The Western region is higher than the North on bridging and marginally higher on bonding.

Both the histories of the regions and their levels of economic development may have contributed to the regional differences in social capital. The peoples of the Central region, which is highest in social capital, have a history of accommodating different groups. This region developed through a process of welcoming and assimilating foreigners, providing them with a local or indigenous name, and integrating them into one of the existing clans. Historical records show, for example, that specific clans from

Table 7.3 (b): Comparisons of value-based social capital in the three regions (Post-Hoc Tests)

Dependent Variable	Regions		Mean differences	Significance
Value-based bonding social capital	Central	Western	0.60	0.001
		Northern	1.05	0.000
	Western	Northern	0.45	0.067
Value-based bridging social capital	Central	Western	-0.07	0.929
		Northern	0.70	0.001
	Western	Northern	0.77	0.004
Combined bonding and bridging social capital	Central	Western	0.52	0.067
		Northern	1.75	0.000
	Western	Northern	1.23	0.000

neighbouring kingdoms such as Bunyoro, integrated into the Central region locally known as Buganda. The higher level of social capital in the Central region and the low level in the Northern region also parallel the relative levels of economic development in the regions, according to national statistics.

In this chapter as well as in Chapter 3, we suggested, in line with the social capital literature, that effective actions that promote escape from poverty are more prevalent in regions that enjoy higher levels of social capital. We now examine this implicit hypothesis by examining data on behaviours that promote well-being. These behaviours include joining projects to master one's environment, joining projects to help others, and joining projects to improve standard of living (see Chapter 6). In Table 6.6 of Chapter 6, we reported that the Central region scored higher than the other two on the level of each of these three behaviours. This is consistent with the findings for regional differences in social capital reported here in Tables 7.3 (a,b).

Another index of the level of social capital is the number of associations or projects found in a locality. Associations are a vehicle for sharing information and solving the problems that face the community. The presence of active associations points to the presence of active and productive citizens. As a second measure of the level of social capital in each district, we asked the respondents to list the number of associations and projects in their locality. The first and second columns of Table 7.4 reveal that, based on the presence of associations, the three districts from the Central region enjoy the highest level of social capital while the two Western districts have the lowest.

A third aspect of social capital is the presence of new settlers in the community. Newcomers may form a bridge between the locals and the outside world and may thereby bring in new ideas. We examined this bridging aspect of social capital by identifying the percentage of respondents in each district who had immigrated to that district rather than being born there. The third and fourth columns of Table 7.4 indicate

Table 7.4: Social capital in the study districts as indicated by number of associations and by the presence of immigrants

Region	District	No. of other associations known to project members	Rank	% Immigrants	Rank
Western	Bushenyi n=21	6	6.5	21	4
	Kabale n=24	6	6.5	17	5
Northern	Arua n=21	12	4	10	6
	Nebbi n=29	10	5	3	7
Central	Mukono n=70	26	1	84	1
	Masaka n=80	24	2	66	3
	Mpigi n=39	16	3	67	2

that the districts from the Central region also have a higher social capital based on percentage of immigrants. In contrast to the findings for associations, however, the Western region showed greater social capital than the Northern region, based on this indicator.

All of the indicators of social capital examined here suggest that the Central region should be the most economically developed among the three regions we studied. Indeed, national statistics on poverty and wealth are consistent with this expectation.

The easier it is for residents of a community to join development projects, the greater the likelihood that social capital will be available. This is because openness of projects allows new members into the group, members who are potential sources of new ideas or bridging capital. We examined openness of the projects by asking about whether people had to have particular qualifications in order to join. Specifically, we asked whether it was necessary for people to come from particular groups in order to be accepted for participation: from a particular tribe, religion, village, age group, or country. Respondents answered yes or no regarding each of these five types of groups. The more limited the accessibility of a project, that is, the more it was restricted to certain groups, the more closed we considered the project to be. The fewer the qualifications required, the more open the project and therefore the more the likelihood that bridging social capital would be available.

Table 7.5 (p.132) reports the percentage of respondents in each district who reported that people could join the project in question regardless of whether they came from a particular group or not. Thus, in Bushenyi, for example, all respondents said that a person could not join the project unless he or she came from a particular tribe, religion, and village, but 60% said that people from any age group could join. In Kabale, the questions about tribe, village, and country were not relevant, but respondents said that

Table 7.5: Percent of respondents in each district who said the project was open to people from any tribe, religion, village, age group, or country

Region	District	Type of group				
		Tribe	**Religion**	**Village**	**Age group**	**Country**
Western	Bushenyi	0	0	0	60	75
	Kabale	-	0	-	0	-
Northern	Arua	27	31	22	41	19
	Nebbi	33	10	51	28	21
Central	Mpigi	64	87	100	100	23
	Mukono	77	97	81	98	13
	Masaka	100	100	68	76	0
	F	19	73	11	22	2.8
	df	6,237	6,238	6.237	6,248	6,239
	p<	.001	.001	.001	.001	.012

participation in a project was barred to those not of the appropriate region and age group.

As Table 7.5 shows, the projects in the districts from the Central region were perceived as the most open. An analysis of variance across the districts, separately for all five types of group, revealed significant differences in the openness of the projects. With regard to every type of group except country, the projects in the districts from the Central region were more open than those from the other districts. Thus, in this analysis as in all of the other quantitative analyses reported in this chapter, the Central region stands out as the one in which social capital is highest.

Qualitative assessments of social capital and its implications for escaping poverty

We now present qualitative data related to social capital in order to illustrate how social capital has assisted individuals to escape poverty. We present and analyse a set of cases in which individuals successfully moved away from poverty. In addition to the text narrative, we organise the data in matrix form (Miles & Huberman, 1994). We utilise an event-listing format because we are interested in how social capital impacts specifically on what people and communities do or do not do. We also use a causal network approach that arranges the actions presented in the matrix in a chronological order that approximates causal relationships.

We present the data for each project in a separate matrix. We present the actions that each individual performed when attempting to deal with poverty-related problems. We then rearrange these actions in a social capital matrix. At the end of the descriptive presentation, we present two causal networks: the project activity network and the corresponding social capital network. The purpose of both networks is to summarise all the data described and discussed in the preceding sections. All cases are selected in such a way as to demonstrate the relevance of social capital in individual and community development. The first set of cases comprises two bottom-up associations that were founded by women and focused on crop farming. The second is a combination of top-down and bottom-up associations that utilised micro-finance in distributive trade.

Moving out of poverty through crop farming

The first set of cases we analyse belong to an organisation known as Twegombe that was founded by Hajati Kalema. They are described in detail in Chapter 5. Here we re-examine them to identify the role played by social capital in their success.

All five cases are built around a focal individual, Hajati Kalema, who moved to a new community after the guerrilla war of 1981-1986 and brought with her new techniques for crop farming. At that time, community members were struggling to eke out a living from their saline soil. To their surprise, they discovered that the newcomer enjoyed immediate success. Part of the village thought that she was a miracle worker who was using supernatural powers to get bumper crops. Some people holding this view assumed that she was a witch who had been excommunicated from her village because only a witch could succeed where everyone else was failing.

Cases 31, 36, 37, 60 and 62, described in Chapter 5 and summarised in Table 7.6 (pp. 134-135) , provide examples of how bridging social capital works. Case 31 was a widow who had suffered financially during her husband's illness. Case 36 was a villager who recognised that Hajati had knowledge to share. Case 37 was a friendly neighbour and Case 62 another immigrant to the community. Hajati's 'bridging' motives varied from case to case. She approached the widow (31) because she wanted to help her financially; she approached her neighbour (37) because she wanted to reach the minimum number of persons needed to form an association. Case 62 is a good example of Hajati's egalitarian behaviour in helping a neighbour who was at first reluctant to undertake agricultural work. Case 36 demonstrates the role of what we have referred to as conversational patterns: A curious individual, hearing what others in the village were saying, decided to find out for herself what Hajati was up to. This action gave Hajati the opportunity she had been looking for to interest her neighbours in what she had been planning to do. Table 7.6 is a social capital matrix of these cases.

We now summarise the causal events relevant to these cases (see Table 5.2, Chapter 5 for more detail). The narratives reveal three constraints on action due to underlying causes-poor soils, lack of motivation to engage in crop farming, and lack of land. These constraining causes kept the inhabitants of the village in poverty until Hajati Kalema successfully intervened in their situation. Her intervention built upon various types of social capital. She served as a bridge to knowledge from outside the community. She had leverage because she knew what was needed to deal with poor soil and how to tell others how to do so. She also provided bonding social support by giving a helping hand whenever she could.

Case 62 in Table 7.6 clearly demonstrates the influence of social capital in a community. It shows that social capital may be exercised at the individual level and not only at the community level. In this case Hajati, the individual behind the changes in this village, was apparently more significant than general community capital. We next reinterpret the events that took place in Twegombe in terms of the social capital exercised.

As noted earlier, weak bridges are connections that people or communities use to learn new ways of behaving and living that are unavailable from their regular circle of

Table 7.6: Social capital analysis of Twegombe Women's Association

Case	Individual bridging capital Weak bridge	Leveraging capital = one knows what to do	Conversational patterns	Networking	Premeditated volunteerism	Associational life	Bonding, reciprocity, trust, social support
60	Settles in new area: Lwadda in 1987.	Practices modern agricultural methods.	Hears what people say about her and decides to deal with it.	Moves around the village looking for women to form an association.	Forms an association to help others so that she could live in peace.	Joins Environmental Alert.	
36	New household headed by Hajati Kalema settles in Lwadda in 1987 soon after the Civil War.	Engages in crop farming with outstanding yields.	New settlers become talk of the village since all other families have low yields.	Respondent visits Hajati for the purpose of befriending her and learning her secrets.	Hajati welcomes her and explains what she does.	They form a new association, Twegombe, in 1992.	

37	Hajati approaches her to form an association and to explain its advantages.	Hajati trains the volunteers in modern agricultural methods. Hajati finds various trainers.	Hajati asks respondent to bring a volunteer.	Hajati brings 4 volunteers. Twegombe is formed with 6 volunteers.		Twegombe grows to 25 volunteers.	
31				Respondent observed women learning new activities at Hajati's.	Hajati approached her to join.		Hajati approached her to join.
62	Visits sister-in-law, finds gathering of women and asks what they are doing.	Hajati teaches her how to use manure.	Learns about Twegombe.		She is approached and encouraged by Hajati to join.	Becomes a member, agrees and pays the dues.	She collects cow dung from the neighbour and from Hajati. Finds crop farming hard but persists and succeeds with one garden then three.

contacts. A bridge is weak when the contacts between the people in question are few and infrequent. Hajati Kalema served as such a bridge in the village to which she moved. She was a stranger bringing previously unavailable information that was instrumental in assisting inhabitants to move out of poverty. Bridges are strong when contacts within the community are constant and intense. Such contacts prevent communities from seeking or obtaining experiences from the wider world. It is these experiences that serve as new inputs to solve a problem. Hajati's activities illustrate the role of weak bridges in innovation. Hajati's arrival in Lwadda village created a weak bridge into the community which Case 36 and other members of Twegombe used to solve the problem that had kept them without sufficient food to feed their families.

Hajati's leverage was her volunteering personality coupled with her skills in crop farming. She was particularly effective at turning poor and rocky soils into fertile ones. Case 62 shows that Hajati was also a kindly person who would come to the aid of a neighbour when she needed support. For instance, she gave people some of her seeds to plant in their garden and some of her cow dung to create manure.

The catalyst for the formation of Twegombe was the general conversation about Hajati's achievements that drew attention to them in the village. This prompted Case 36 to visit Hajati and confirm what she had heard. Her other intention was to learn how to do whatever it was that Hajati had succeeded in doing while everyone else in the village had failed. Hajati and the inquisitive woman struck-up a productive relationship. They arranged to identify hard-working women who could form the core of an association intended to help individuals escape poverty through co-operative action. Hajati's motives in working to form this voluntary association may be characterised as premeditated volunteerism. That is, she chose to help others succeed as she was succeeding in order to serve her own interests as well. She was concerned to find a way to live peacefully in her new village and reasoned that she could do this by helping.

The example of another development association, Akwata Rural Development Association (ARDA), demonstrates the role of associations in helping people escape from poverty. ARDA was formed as a mirror image of Twegombe. One of the founders of ARDA had earlier visited Hajati Kalema and found that the problems Twegombe was trying to solve were similar to the ones in her own village, Sisa, twenty miles away. Because this person apparently did not have the same skills as Hajati, she relied much more on outside associations than Hajati had in building Twegombe.

Again we present a set of cases (33,34,35,53 in Table 7.7 ; see Chapter 5 for details) that illustrate the role of the individual in the diffusion of ideas. The diffusion agent in the formation of ARDA was Mrs Mbaziira. She followed the same route as Hajati Kalema, gathering people who were interested and demonstrating how they would profit by joining an association. Like Hajati, she knew that associations are necessary to succeed. ARDA linked the group to outside groups such as Twegombe, Vision 2000 and UNDP. Mrs Mbaziira took others to meet her own source of knowledge and demonstrated that she had profited from the experience with Twegombe. Case 34 illustrates the positive outcomes of the efforts of ARDA. After she had learned the farming methods taught through ARDA, she gave up her trade in Kampala to concentrate on what she had learned. Case 53 stated explicitly that what she learned through ARDA had improved her harvests so much that she ccould now feed her

Table 7.7: Social capital interpretation of ARDA

Case capital:	Bridging capital:	Leveraging patterns Weak bridge	Conversational Knowing what to do	Networking volunteerism	Premeditated	Associational life	Bonding, reciprocity trust, social support
33	Approaches respondent to join ARDA in order to learn sustainable agriculture.	ARDA invites Vision 2000 to train ARDA members including respondent.	Approaches respondent to to join ARDA in order to learn sustainable agriculture.	Mrs Mbaziira visits Hajati Kalema in Matugga.		She returns and co-founds ARDA.	
34	Arranges for UNDP trainers to come and train.	Elderly male teaches her what he had learned in ARDA.		Approached by an elderly ARDA male.	Now convinced she gives up trade.		Elderly male teaches her what he had learned in ARDA.
35	She too mobilises others including husband to see for themselves.	The friend learns how Hajati uses locally made manure to get good yields.		A family friend visits Hajati of Twegombe.	Friend makes arrangement for her to visit Hajati.	When they return they form their own association: ARDA.	She too mobilises others including husband to see for themselves.
53	She invites respondent to join ARDA in order for her to learn new ways of crop farming.	Her harvests improve and she has food to spare and to sell in the market.				Friend joins ARDA and learns new ways of crop farming.	

Table 7.8: Event Listing: 'Get Together' Women's Project

Case	Event 1	Event 2	Event 3	Event 4	Event 5	Event 6
142	Co-founds 'Get Together'.	Learns from the town Mayor that FINCA would assist them with finance.	Told to increase membership to between 20 & 30.	Members of Get Together mobilise others.	Apply for loans from FINCA and receive them.	
141	Buys one-week-old chicks.	Hears about 'Get Together' from a friend.	Tries to join in order to get financial assistance from FINCA	Denied entry because she does not have a viable source of income yet.	Told to reapply when chicks are laying eggs.	Reapplies and succeeds.
140	Respondent is a market vendor.	Has been searching for capital to expand business.	Learns about FINCA and its relationship to 'Get Together'.	Joins 'Get Together' in order to access FINCA loans.		
139	Wants to expand her second-hand clothes business.	Learns about 'Get Together' which is giving financial assistance to women.	Joins and told to start saving in 'Get Together'.	Later is given loan from FINCA.		
138	Respondent makes samosas and supplies them to Mukono Town.	Tries to secure a loan to expand her business without success.	Member of 'Get Together' who is a friend informs her about the association.	Learns that she fulfils conditions for securing a loan.	Joins 'Get Together' and secures a FINCA loan.	
137	Sells foodstuff in the Evening Market.	Learns of FINCA and 'Get Together' through the Mayor.	Joins 'Get Together' to secure loans from FINCA and learn other skills such as basket making.			

many children and she had food to spare for the market. Thus ARDA has helped her to escape poverty. Table 7.7 presents the events that led to the formation of ARDA in terms of the social capital involved.

In sum, both Twegombe and ARDA were formed and functioned in accordance with the model of social capital outlined at the beginning of the chapter.

Escaping poverty through micro-finance

The members of the next set of projects are small-scale entrepreneurs who rely on micro-finance institutions for credit. Until they joined associations, they could not raise enough capital to expand their businesses. Expansion here means making the businesses profitable enough for the proceeds to meet basic necessities. The experiences of these people are summarised in Tables 7.8, 7.9, 7.10, 7.11 and 7.12.

Table 7.8 displays the sequence of events in the lives of a group of women who sought to escape poverty. It specifies the constraints they faced and how they overcame them. The key to many of the women's problems was a lack of information regarding what to do. Several women were already engaged in small income generating activities that they had wanted to expand but had been unsuccessful. Case 142 took the lead by helping to form an association, but the objectives of the association were not clearly articulated. The town's mayor helped the floundering association because he knew what the women needed and how they could get it. He was able to convert his enthusiasm into practical results because of the existence of the 'Get Together' association. Without it, his efforts would have taken longer to yield fruit because the international NGO that promotes micro-finance (FINCA) operates only where beneficiaries are already in viable groups. Building on 'Get Together' facilitated reaching the required minimum group size of 20.

Table 7.9 (pp.140-141) describes the role of both individual and community social capital in the events leading to the development and success of this project. Members who joined Get Together and were able to secure loans from FINCA learned from friends or acquaintances about these associations. These contacts are another example of the weak bridges that are the key to rural innovation. The founder of Get Together drew upon the knowledge of another weak bridge in the person of the mayor with whom she did not regularly have contact. The mayor can be considered the person with leverage. He was the one who knew what to do and who linked the women to FINCA. Other people played this role after the association established itself. Case 138 describes an acquaintance who informed her about 'Get Together' and about FINCA and what she was required to do. This friend was a member of 'Get Together' and had already secured a loan from FINCA through 'Get Together'.

Premeditated volunteerism features significantly in all the social capital events and actions. The table makes clear why all the actors, except the mayor and the founder, joined 'Get Together'. However, the complete narratives from our respondents reveal more. 'Get Together' was founded around the time of a political campaign. For the mayor, bringing development to the town was a way of boosting his chances of being re-elected. He was able to do this by linking 'Get Together' with FINCA. Had 'Get Together' not existed, the mayor himself would have had to mobilise women to form associations before they could access loans. By exploiting the community social capital

Table 7.9: Social capital analysis of 'Get Together' Women's Project

Case	Individual bridging capital Weak bridge	Leveraging capital = one knows what to do	Networking	Premeditated volunteerism	Associational life	Bonding, reciprocity, trust, social support
142		Mayor tells them that FINCA would assist them with finance.	Co-founds 'Get Together'.	Members of 'Get Together' mobilised others.	'Get To-gether' presence of FINCA in the area.	Told to increase number of membership to between 20-30.
141	Hears about 'Get To-gether' from a friend.	Denied entry because she does not have a viable source of income yet.		Tries to join in order to get financial assist-ance from FINCA.		

140			Learns about FINCA and its relationship to 'Get Together'.	Joins Get Together in order to access FINCA loans.
139		Told to start saving in Get Together	Learns that 'Get Together' is giving financial assistance to women.	Joins and is told to start saving in 'Get Together'.
138	Member of Get Together and friend informs respondent about the association.	Respondent learns that she meets conditions for securing a loan.		Joins and secures loan from FINCA.
137	Learns of FINCA and Get Together through the Mayor.			Joins 'Get Together' to secure loans from FINCA and learn other skills such as basket making.

Table 7.10: Twekembe Balunzi Group

Case	Event 1	Event 2	Event 3	Event 4	Event 5	Event 6
125	Respondent sells second-hand clothes.	Looks for credit to expand business without success.	Informed by a friend of a group project known as Twekembe Balunzi Group without giving details.	Searches for more information from other people.	Learns of the conditions for qualifying and takes steps to meet them.	Joins the group and accesses a loan from MED-NET.
126	Runs a small scale enterprise.	Looks for credit to expand business without success.	Approached by an individual who with others was trying to form a group in order to access credit.	Registered immediately and accesses credit.		
127	Respondent has small scale business.	A friend joins Twekembe and asks her to join also.	Respondent sceptical of the promises.	Approached by one of the original founders and is convinced.	Joins in order to access credit.	
128	Respondent operating a small retail shop in Mukono.	Joined the Burial Credit groups which failed because of mismanagement.	Husband prevented her from joining any other group.	Informed by a friend about Twekembe and its intentions.	Joined secretly and trained for two months with MED-NET.	
129	Was one of three small scale entrepreneurs without a means of expanding their business.	Approached Poverty Alleviation Programme for a loan but failed to get credit because of stiff conditions.	Learned from an officer from Mukono Town Council about MED-NET which gave loans to groups of (30) people.	They mobilised 28 and formed a group known as Twekembe Kitete Group.		
130	Managing a small poultry project.	Wanted to expand but distrusted borrowing from individuals.	Informally considered forming a group with six other women with various businesses but abandoned the idea because of money for registration.	Approached by three gentlemen trying to set up an association.	Joined the new association happily.	

in his town, in the form of 'Get Together' and FINCA, the mayor promoted his own goal of getting re-elected. At the same time, his actions improved the standard of living of the townspeople, especially members of 'Get Together' whose motive for starting the association had been to access loans for development.

The second association we consider under micro-finance is the Twekembe Balunzi group. Unlike the other groups discussed so far, it was created by three actors. Table 7.10 presents the relevant events.

At the start, a group of men who lacked credit considered setting up an organisation. They were informed by an officer from Mukono Town Council (second actor), however, that viable groups must have a membership of 30. The third actor was a group of seven women who had also been wrestling with the problem of accessing credit. These women knew that they too needed a group, but had failed to form one because they could not raise money for registering an organisation.

Case study 7.1 is a good example of a community that knows how to deal with its problems. Together with Table 7.10, it demonstrates community social capital. Apparently,

Case Study 7.1: Founding Twekembe Balunzi Group

NO:	130
DISTRICT:	MUKONO
SUBCOUNTY:	MUKONO TOWN COUNCIL
VILLAGE:	KITETE

NAME OF PROJECT: TWEKEMBE BALUNZI GROUP

WHY DID YOU JOIN?

Sometime back, women in Kitete Village talked about forming a group. They realised they had various economic activities, which they wanted to undertake, but the problem was lack of capital. Some of the women were engaged in poultry keeping, brick making, business enterprises and others. At this stage, these women neither had a name for the group they wanted to form nor the money to register it. Therefore, the idea was left at that point. The idea began among seven women and the respondent was one of them.

Some time later, what appeared to be a dream became a reality when three gentlemen, Mr Kintu, Ssalongo Sekanga, and Kawonawo, after hearing that MED-NET gives credit to people who have formed groups, decided to mobilise people to form a group. The aim behind the formation of the group was to obtain credit from MED-Net.

The three men approached the respondent, who together with six other women had considered the idea of forming a group similar to what Mr Kintu and the other two men had in mind.

The respondent was involved in poultry keeping which she wanted to boost but did not have the means. She had realised the difficulty of approaching individuals for loans. It involves exposing one's problems and secrets, yet at the end of it all, that individual might not even advance the loan. He /She might later expose those secrets or problems to other people, which is not good. Therefore, the respondent realised that by forming a group, she would receive loans without going through the above-mentioned problems. Thus, when approached by the three men, the respondent was just too happy to join the group.

Table 7.11: Social capital in Twekembe Balunzi Group

Case	Individual bridging capital Weak bridge	Leveraging capital = one knows what to do	Conversational patterns	Networking	Premeditated volunteerism	Associational life	Bonding, reciprocity, trust, social support
125	Informed by a friend of a group project known as Twekembe.	Learns of the conditions for qualifying and takes steps to meet them.		Searches for more information from other people.	Joins the group and accesses a loan from MED-NET.	MED-NET Twekembe.	
126	Approached by an individual trying to form a group.	Registered immediately and accesses credit.			Were trying to form a group in order to access credit.		
127	A friend joins Twekembe and asks her to join also.				Joins in order to access credit.		
129	Learned from an officer from Mukono Town Council about MED-NET which gave loans to groups of (30) people.	Officer knew of MED-NET which gave loans to groups.		Mobilised 28 and formed a group known as Twekembe Kitete Group.			
130	Approached by men trying to set up an association.				Joined the new association happily.		

Table 7.12: Project-target-benefit matrix

Type of Project	Target group	Reason for joining	Service offered	Benefits to members
Twegombe ARDA Crop farming Self help project Bottom-up	Women with poor agricultural yields and so negative attitude. towards farming.	Improve agricultural productivity.	Training in modern agriculture using organic inputs.	Acquired skills improved yields. Changed attitude towards agriculture. Reduced cost of living.
Twekembe Micro-finance Top-down	Low-income earners	Expand business	Credit	Obtained loan. Business expanded.
Balimanya Micro-finance Top-down	Small income earners	Promote individual economic activity.	Credit	Obtained loan. Business expanded.
'Get Together' Micro-finance Top-down	Low income earners	Promote economic activity.	Credit	Obtained loan. Business expanded.
Send-A-Cow Heifer Project Dairy farming Top-down	Needy women	Improve standard of living.	In-calf heifer Training in animal husbandry.	Improved diet. Improved income through selling milk.

the people of Mukono Town were already aware of the specific steps that needed to be taken. Two groups of community members (3 men and 7 women) simultaneously thought of forming an association in order to access credit for the purpose of expanding their businesses. Table 7.11 re-examines Table 7.10 in terms of social capital.

Tables 7.10 and 7.11, when examined concurrently, indicate the role of leverage. All individuals in this group knew what they wanted. Only one required persuading (Case 127). However, few understood how to go about solving the problem of accessing credit in order to expand their businesses. A good example is Case 129, which describes the effort of three individuals. These went to the Poverty Alleviation Programme, a Government/World Bank sponsored project. They failed to secure a loan because they could not meet the stiff conditions. They were, however, saved by an officer from the town council who was knowledgeable about opportunities for micro-financing in the area.

Table 7.10 also includes an example of the familiar pattern in which a person known to a respondent informs her of an opportunity in the locality. Those who give this

Figure 7.1: Event-Causal Network from Narratives

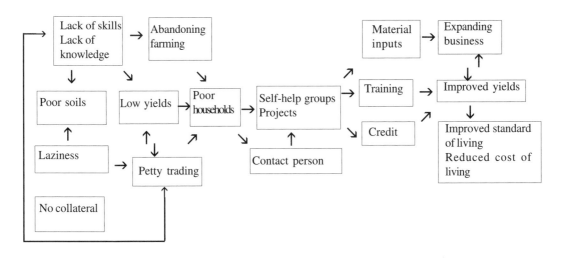

information are often people who will profit if the individual approached takes up the opportunity. The information also contains a clue suggesting what the person approached stands to gain. When this person is still unsure what she will gain, the desired response is never immediate. Only repeated approaches yield the desired outcome. Here the desired outcome is that the person approached joins the association and enables it to reach the necessary size to gain access to credit for all of its members. This dynamic of offering help to others in order to gain for self as well is another example of premeditated volunteerism, the essence of individual social capital.

We now present an explanatory effect matrix that describes several successful projects we studied. It contains limited narratives that allow meaningful analyses. One of projects, the Heifer project, was not included in the diagrams above because it exhibited a pattern similar to those we did include. The information regarding this project in the matrix in Table 7.12 suffices for our analysis.

The matrix summarises project objectives, targets, resources offered, and outcomes for project members. Members either joined existing organisations (top-down) in order to access resources or they created their own organisations (bottom-up) and then sought help. All joined for instrumental reasons such as learning better agricultural methods or access to credit to expand business. All profited from participation.

Several events created poverty and others helped the poor to deal with some of the consequences of poverty. These are described in Figure 7.1. We summarise our analysis with two causal network diagrams. The first concerns poverty and how people tried to escape from it. The second is a demonstration of the social capital events that explain how the poor can successfully move out of poverty.

Four conditions are associated with poverty in the households we visited. First was that individuals who had reached the limits of their capacity to deal with their problems lacked the knowledge of what to do. In the cases of Twegombe and ARDA, people did not know how to increase the fertility of their soils or how to cultivate intensively using

Figure 7.2: Social capital causal-event network in the projects.

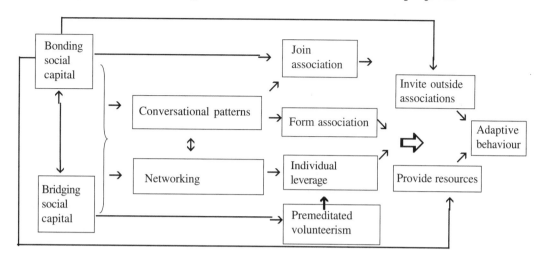

a small space. These people gave up crop farming or spent proportionally little time in farming activities. As a result, these families had to buy food to feed their members, even though they lived in rural or semi-rural areas. The people in distributive trades fared no better. They lacked knowledge of what to do to access credit. Consequently, they remained at the level of petty trading and they, too, could not meet their basic needs. For example, a woman who had a retail shop still had to rely on her husband for many of her basic needs.

In each case, the key to overcoming problems was contact with a person who could show them what to do. The contact person is one who provides leverage and sets in motion a series of activities that, when followed, allow people to move out of poverty. In social capital terms, this individual is a person with leverage. In the case of Twegombe, the founder herself knew enough to organise the needy into an association and to teach them what they needed to know. In other cases, the contact person directed them to societies that had the needed resources. In all the cases, members of the associations reported that they had profited from the experience both financially and materially. Figure 7.2 presents a social capital causal event network. It demonstrates how the kinds of events initiated by people with leverage in the community helped people to improve their standard of living.

Twegombe and ARDA started with networking, conversations, and an individual volunteering to bring others together. ARDA relied on outside organisations, including Twegombe, to bring resources to the members. Twegombe on the other hand, relied more on the skills of an individual. The other projects we visited resembled ARDA in that the contact person linked individuals with those who could provide them with resources. The possibility of doing this depended, in every case, on the prior existence of associations or organisations. For instance, ARDA utilised Vision 2000 and UNDP. Others relied on FINCA, MED-NET and the Send-a-Cow Church Heifer Project. Very similar patterns characterised all the projects we visited. Conversations, networking, and weak bridges provided information to those who sought it. The case of Twegombe is especially interesting because the reason people started talking was because they were suspicious of the newcomer, not because they wished to learn from her. She, however, was not discouraged by people's reaction to her success, deciding instead to bring them together so that they, too, learned how to farm successfully.

We started this chapter by outlining conditions that indicate the presence of social capital in a community. These included trust and reciprocity, premeditated volunteerism, engaging regularly in wide ranging conversation, the ability to form and to belong to a variety of associations, experiencing a sense of equality within a community, and optimism about the locale so that individuals are willing to invest in it. The cases reviewed here provide direct supporting evidence for most of these conditions. A few examples will attest to this assertion.

Optimism: Hajati Kalema experienced difficulties when those who were jealous of her success in crop farming started accusing her of supernatural powers. However, she proactively dealt with the situation by creating an association through which she could bring them closer to her and then teach them how to farm successfully. If Hajati had not been optimistic, she might have considered moving again.

Associations: The central role of associations to join is found most clearly with Twekembe and 'Get Together'. Both of these societies were able to satisfy the needs of their membership by linking them with other resource-endowed organisations in the neighbourhood. Twekembe and 'Get Together' are found in Mukono district. From primary data, this was the district that ranked as number one in the density of associations.

It seems clear from the analysis that two conditions were particularly important for explaining efforts and success in escaping poverty: the presence of weak bridges and premeditated volunteerism. We examine these two conditions in more detail.

Weak bridges: Weak bridges result from weak ties. Whether a tie is weak or strong depends on the intensity of feeling between the individuals in contact or between an individual and a community (see Chapter 5). The strength of a tie is often measured in terms of the frequency with which individuals are prepared to physically interact. Individuals who are linked by strong ties have many things in common. Such ties are unlikely to bring new ideas to a community or to an individual because people already share the knowledge or skills they have. Consequently, bridging capital usually consists of weak ties, as repeatedly illustrated in our analyses. In all cases, respondents obtained the critical new information from friends rather than from relatives with whom they are likely to have close ties. In the case of Hajati, the weak bridge was a relative stranger. In the case of Twekembe, the group of men founders sought to build a network by turning to complete strangers, looking for whoever was interested.

People with whom we are loosely connected are weak bridges. They belong to other groups and live in other environments where we are relative or complete strangers. The new ideas needed to solve the problems we encounter are likely to come from such circles. People who change homes or jobs create weak ties. Strangers in a community are a potential source of social capital because their ties are weak. The presence of many, varied formal and informal organisations in a community also promotes weak ties. It creates opportunities for people to interact with a wide range of others.

Because it is impossible to have very many close friends, this opportunity does not lead to many strong friendships. But it promotes acquiring a large number of acquaintances who can serve as weak bridges. Thus, the more opportunities there are to interact with people in different organisations, the more people there are who can serve as weak bridges. These are the ones with leverage, those who may know what to do in the face of problems that the close group cannot solve. As Granovetter (1973) noted, the absence of weak ties does more damage to a locality than the absence of strong ties.

Premeditated volunteerism: The importance and nature of premeditated volunteerism were best illustrated by Hajati Kalema. It entails deciding deliberately to help others out of both self-serving and other-serving motives. It involves helping behaviour that requires a long-term commitment and extends over time. It is not a spontaneous, emotion-driven response to the apparent need of others. Non-spontaneous volunteers are high on social responsibility, internal locus of control, and are responsive to the suffering of others. They exhibit a capacity for extensive relationships (egalitarian) within and outside their close circles. Hajati Kalema exhibited all these characteristics. We have not described her characteristic of internal locus of control. She exhibited an internal locus of control in response to the villagers who were jealous of her and threatened to ostracise her. Rather than blame them for making her life unbearable and throwing up her hands as a person who sees her fate controlled by the external environment, she believed that her own actions could change the situation.

Spontaneous volunteerism occurs in situations with strong cues that leave no option but to help. If an adult sees a child running into the road, for example, almost all would shout for the child to stop and try to grab him or her, if possible. Non-spontaneous, premeditated volunteerism occurs in situations with weak cues that give one time to decide whether or not to help. In such situations people may weigh what they themselves will gain or lose by helping.

We conclude by noting relations among the strength of bridges, situational cues, and premeditated volunteerism. In close relationships, bridges are strong and people know what is expected of them by others. That is, the situational cues guiding behaviour are strong and nothing new is likely to develop. When ties are loose and bridges weak, there is more freedom of action. Situational cues are weak and do not dictate appropriate behaviour. This allows actors to select the course of action that they think is good for themselves and/or for the community. If they freely choose to act to benefit the community, their free choice enhances their commitment to their act of volunteering and promotes continuity and persistence in the face of obstacles.

Conclusion

This chapter examined how people mobilise social capital to escape from poverty. Our analysis of how the components of social capital affected the successful projects we studied revealed that villagers trusted each other, took risks for one another, and performed acts of reciprocity. Both initiators of projects and early adopters engaged in premeditated volunteerism aimed at serving their own individual interests by enabling the community.

The qualitative examples discussed here were drawn from the Central region. Similar examples can be found in the other regions. We chose the Central region because, of the three regions in which we collected data, this region had the highest score on all our measures of quantitative social capital.

Unique to our quantitative analyses was the specification of shared cultural value orientations as a form of social capital. The qualitative analysis did not directly address the contribution of these value orientations to the actions of those involved in the projects. An examination of the motives and actions of the key actors, however, suggests that prevailing value orientations were indeed important sources of influence. For example, the cultural emphasis on egalitarianism in their society supported the bonding activities of Hajati Kalema and Mrs Mbaziira of ARDA. It justified building networks of interdependent women who treated one another as morally worthy and undertook voluntary cooperative action. Similarly, the cultural emphasis on mastery gave legitimacy to the bold initiatives and risks that central figures in the projects undertook in the face of inertia and even opposition in their surroundings. An in depth analysis of the role of cultural orientations as a form of social capital must await research designed for that purpose. These examples show, however, that people's shared cognitions, including the values prevailing in their society, constitute a form of social capital.

8

Towards a Social Psychology
of Development

This chapter describes in more general terms the person trying to move out of poverty, the individual-in-development, or the social psychological individual. We use this second label in order to emphasise the need to understand how the poor interact continuously with significant others, deliberately forming and drawing upon social networks to ensure their own survival. Among the deliberate actions of the poor that must be understood are the short-term tactical decisions they make and the longer-term strategies they employ to preserve their limited resources or improve their situation. To assist the poor person through appropriate policies and strategies, we propose a social psychology of development. It is designed to be relevant to understanding the onset of behavioural poverty and the initiation of behavioural well-being among Ugandan and other African individuals. This social psychology of development makes use of tools in a number of well-developed areas in psychology and in other social sciences such as sociology, anthropology and African philosophical anthropology. Below we outline the tenets we have found relevant in the study reported above.

Eight tentative tenets underlying the social psychology of development

1.The onset of poverty is traceable to poverty carriers, that is, to actions that an individual or community performs or that are enacted upon them; actions that adversely affect the optimal utilisation of productive resources.
When investigating the history of poverty-carrying actions, the social psychology of development focuses both on the actors' own actions and on actions that outside agents have performed upon the actors. Action Theory, as adopted by Frese and Zapf (1994), provides tools for analysing the poverty carrying action that actors initiate. The theory suggests that the anticipated outcomes of activities serve as goals that determine the kind of activity that should be undertaken. It recognises that there are prerequisites to actions such as motives and abilities, but it focuses on the action-goal relationship. Goals give direction to actions-the 'smallest unit of behaviour that is related to a conscious goal' (Hacker, 1986, p. 73 from Frese & Zap, 1994, p. 274). Conscious goals provide direction to action through such activities as planning, executing the plan, and receiving feedback. Goals provide the motivation for actors to persist in the face of barriers, and to seek out and organise goal-oriented information.

Chapters 4 through 7 described individuals in Uganda who faced barriers and setbacks. Some we met failed to overcome these barriers and therefore sank deeper into poverty. But some managed to surmount the barriers. Because we are especially interested in learning how individuals overcome barriers, we have focused on what these people do, who they are, and who are the people with whom they interact.

151

2. What individuals can do is determined or prescribed by cultural learning.
Cultural learning refers to what individuals have learned through socialisation in the community and can do in co-operation with others. The better the quality and the greater the quantity of what community members can do co-operatively, the more developed and less poverty-stricken the community will be. Like Vygotsky (1978), we equate cultural learning with community learning and development. Cultural learning is the cornerstone of the social psychology of development.

Vygotsky describes cultural learning as attainment of higher-level mental functions, such as selective attention, verbal thought and reasoning, and logical memory. These functions entail voluntary control over one's own behaviour rather than the automatic responses of lower level functions. Higher-level mental functions make possible forethought and conscious planning to deal with problems. For instance, contrast the responses of people and animals to a raging fire. Using lower level functions, animals usually react automatically by running away. People may utilise planning, selective attention and reasoning and therefore stay by the fire because they started it deliberately to get rid of refuse or to celebrate an occasion around a bonfire – or to find a way of putting it out safely. Consider another instance using logical memory. A baby's crying serves as a stimulus to remind her mother to feed her. The mother's action is driven by lower level memory in response to the stimulus environment. On the other hand, the mother may plan a schedule to feed her baby every six hours. She may record the exact feeding hours in her diary and feed the baby when six hours have elapsed, even if the baby does not cry. Here, the mother controls her own behaviour using logical memory.

Higher-level mental functions characterise all people who are socialised. However, the content to which the functions apply may differ from community to community. Consider selective attention. People everywhere pay attention to events that are meaningful to them and ignore those that are not. However, the specific situations and history of a community determine what is meaningful and what is not. Consequently, Vygotsky refers to higher-level mental functions as cultural functions. They are influenced by prior experience or history in the form of activities carried out with parents, elders, peers and superiors and depend on the tools such as specific languages, gestures, and material technology available to carry out activities. The fact that prior experience, interpersonal activity, and tools are situation specific must be taken into account when designing learning for development.

3. The central mechanism for cultural or community learning is the zone of proximal development-the distance between the level of development people actually attain based on independent problem solving and the level they could potentially attain through problem solving under adult guidance or in collaboration with more capable peers.
In practice, the zone of proximal development operates as a learning network. Interpersonal learning occurs only when there is potential for growth within a person's network of social relations. If people can find no new collaborative activity from which to learn, the zone of proximal development for a particular individual or community decays. This is the case when all collaborative activity repeats the same routines. Of

course, newcomers find these activities novel and they develop their mental capacities to the level at which the community can reward them. Thus the zone of proximal development sets the limits for growth.

The zone of proximal development may atrophy and no longer constitute a network with new resources for learning. In this case, interpersonal learning or development by the individual or community ceases and stagnation sets in. Articulating the nature of failing or thriving zones of proximal development in a community is the starting point for understanding the onset of poverty and for initiating a return to development. To stop decay in the zone of proximal development, it must be rejuvenated or revitalised. We briefly discuss two ways this can occur (see Chapter 4).

The first is through so called 'weak bridges' over which knowledge can pass. These bridges are people who are connected to more than one group or community and can span the gaps between them. They are not in daily contact with the group whose zone of proximal development has decayed. Their connections with this group are sufficiently weak that they have opportunities to acquire higher mental functions or cultural learning that are different from that of the group.

People who serve as weak bridges typically possess three personal attributes: personal initiative, innovativeness and risk-taking. Personal initiative refers to the behaviour syndrome of taking a proactive and self-starting approach to work, going beyond what is formally required, and pursuing long-term life goals that promote persistence in the face of barriers and setbacks (Frese, et al, 1996, p. 38). Innovation refers to a social process that combines generating new ideas and involving others in implementing them. Although a person can be creative and generate new ideas alone, the implementation of ideas typically depends upon the approval, support and resources of others (Axtell et al., 2000). The risk-taking attribute is important because initiating and innovating often entail deviation from normative ways of doing things and are therefore risky.

The second way to revitalise the zone of proximal development is to create and utilise so-called "structural holes", gaps between discrete networks within a community. Different associations in the same community may be disconnected and have different missions and objectives. The presence of such associations in a community provides opportunities for evolving different cultural 'learnings' that are also accessible to individuals with the weak bridge characteristics just mentioned.

4. The dominant cultural interface-the meeting of distinct institutions and cultural elements that people defend or reject-in a zone of proximal development determines the effectiveness of the learning that takes place.

The cultural interface is an interactive environment in which two or more people with different cultural commitments come together to transact business, exchange information, learn from one another and so on. Cultural learning does not necessarily proceed smoothly. Our individual-in-development approach views people as embedded in contexts composed of institutions and cultural elements that they are predisposed to defend or to reject. The critical elements in these contexts are the patterned beliefs, values and practices that people take for granted, accept and defend or overlook or reject.

When people or groups in a community identify with or are committed to institutions and cultural elements that are incompatible, some of the interfaces will be conflictual.

This may undermine the effectiveness of cultural learning in the zone of proximal development. The impact of cultural interfaces on the outcome of transactions among individuals and groups is proportional to the cultural/social distance between the parties to the interaction. The conflict between cultural interfaces may be due to the different commitments of community members (endogenous), but it may also result from alien cultural elements imported from outside the community (exogenous).

The precise nature of the culturally patterned beliefs, values and practices in a community may be obscure or barely recognised. So it is important to seek out and actively identify the cultural elements and institutions in order to specify zones of proximal development and plan effective development projects. Just as it is imperative to articulate the zone of proximal development in order to understand the individual-in-development, it is equally critical to map out and verbalise the cultural interface. Policy makers and project designers should try to articulate the cultural interfaces they expect to emerge if their plans are carried out.

5. Those who wish to assist the individual-in-development in Africa must pay attention to numerous generic but endogenous cultural interfaces including the economy of affection, women's heavier work burden, and anti-scientific reasoning about causality.

Each of these cultural elements produces problematic interfaces when development projects introduce different sets of beliefs or assumptions.

a) The economy of affection is a well-researched endogenous cultural interface (Hyden, 1983, Illfe 1983). It refers to the belief that individuals' achievements belong to those around them, especially to the extended family and friends. Consequently, successful individuals are duty-bound to share what they achieve. This cultural interface derives from the pre-colonial cultural practice of neighbours and relatives coming together to help individuals build their houses, prepare the ground for planting or help in the harvest. In return, these neighbours were felt to have a claim on the products of the collaborative activity. This practice of mutually supportive activity is fast dying out. However, the claims on others for joint consumption have persisted.

b) The allocation of roles to men and women in Africa continues to impose as much as 65% of the work required in a community on women. Despite major attempts to reduce patriarchy through policies and affirmative action legislation, this interface persists, probably because men continue to dominate the positions of authority in most communities.

c) The causation interface is the cultural interface least researched by social scientists. African philosophers have asserted that the fundamental religiosity of Africans leads them to explain what happens in life by invoking fate or supernatural forces rather than scientific reasoning about causality. This marginalises sustained scientific and intellectual efforts. Consequently Africans tend to promote and use the simple technologies they have inherited rather than developing or adopting scientifically-based technologies that produce more efficient and effective solutions.

6. Social capital is a harmonious cultural interface that can stem the spread of behavioural poverty and aid in the initiation of behavioural well-being.
Social capital refers to shared cognitions that people choose to sustain through structures such as roles, rules, and networks. Social capital is a congruent combination of shared cognitions, institutionalised overt behaviour and expectations that motivate continued shared cognitions. It is expressed in such things as trust in societal institutions and in other people. A study of the individual-in-development should clarify the social capital that exists in the community because social capital is instrumental to development.

7. The process of escaping behavioural poverty is one of interaction among people who are linked in a network of cultural learners.
The onset of poverty may result from the failing actions of an individual. But only actions taken in interaction with others can lead to an escape from poverty. Thus, the process of escaping poverty is essentially one of interaction rather than action. Networks bring together individuals who share a vision and who stay together as they continue to share the vision. They also agree that they will freely disband if the vision sharing disappears. Networks utilise weak bridges to span structural holes and promote the learning and development of the individuals they chain together. By adhering to the following principles, network members can ensure successful learning (Willis, 1994):
a) Sharply project the vision that holds the people together to prevent them from exercising their voluntary and well understood right to withdraw. This will happen when the leader allows good ideas to germinate from any member of the network.
b) Encourage, promote, and manage intellectual and cognitive restlessness, demonstrated through heated debate among members that keeps the network focused sharply on the environment or ecosystem.
c) Seek and maintain consensus on substantive issues of process and content rather than on detail.
d) Pay attention to gate-keeping and maintenance functions in order to assure the relevance of each member to the network.
e) Persuade members to join wholeheartedly and appreciate that networks are as good as their last success or failure.
f) Continuously scan the internal and external environments for the purpose of adapting to changing circumstances.
g) Provide order in the 'shifting sand' of network relations.

Applying the social psychological model of development
We have suggested that, in order to develop successful methods for alleviating behavioural poverty, it is necessary to uncover the specific acts in the daily lives of the poor that lead to the outcomes typically viewed as indicators of poverty (i.e., level of income, housing conditions, calorie consumption). If these poverty-carrying acts are identified, academics and practitioners can more easily design policies to target them directly. Using an action framework, we identified several poverty carriers in the study reported here. Among the acts that produce or perpetuate poverty is selling one's piece of land, one's own labour, or one's children's labour. We have found these to be

strategic acts that firmly place individuals and households on the road to poverty. They must change if individuals are to escape behavioural poverty.

A way to identify such retrogressive and poverty-causing actions is to examine communities' zones of proximal development. Using qualitative methods, we uncovered several zones of proximal development in the communities we studied. Most outstanding was the zone associated with Hajati's Twegombe and the villager who befriended Hajati Kalema (see Chapters 5 and 7). Our analyses revealed that these two people accurately identified an atrophying zone of proximal development. They revitalised this zone of development by generating the network of linked individuals known as Twegombe (the literal translation is 'let us admire for the purpose of learning'). They provided this network with specific and achievable objectives centred around creating food security in the community. The revitalised zone of proximal development served as a centre for cultural learning, for acquiring higher mental functions such as employing mulching, organising people into productive groups, and managing finances in the home by exploiting subsistence crop farming as a source of income. The success of the revitalised zone of proximal development led to the founding of other voluntary associations to deal with problems similar to those that brought Twegombe into existence (see figure 5.2 Chapter 5).

The formation of Twegombe and the other zones of proximal development it inspired in distant villages (ARDA, Twekembe and 'Get Together', at least 32 kilometres away) demonstrates other aspects of the social psychology of development we propose. Two points stand out. First is the way an individual (Hajati Kalema) utilised an existing structural hole to promote her own development and then created other structural holes. She took advantage of the Environmental Alert organisation as a source of interpersonal learning. After internalising this learning, she took upon herself voluntarily to plan and create Twegombe in order to remain peacefully in her chosen village. Twegombe's success in achieving results, while using simple and accessible technology, created a unique model. It served as a structural hole that others could exploit for their own development. This was done first by Mrs Mbaziira of ARDA and later by others from ARDA and elsewhere.

This case also exemplifies another cornerstone of the social psychological model we propose, the cultural interface. It illustrates two interfaces. The first is the causation interface (see tenet 7c). This refers to the anti-scientific cultural orientation prevalent in much of Africa. As we saw, the villagers threatened Hajati with excommunication because she succeeded where everyone else had failed. They thought it was not humanly possible to succeed with crop farming in the village, hence only a witch could succeed. Hajati knew that the food insecurity in the village was caused by personal failures rather than by divine intervention. What saved her from expulsion was another villager. This woman also had the capacity to see the failure as caused by the actions of the village residents rather than by powerful and evil others. She served as a bridge, demonstrating in her actions the personal attributes of initiative and risk taking. The shared beliefs of these two women gave them the basis for dealing with the causation interface and creating the new zone of proximal development that came to be known as Twegombe.

The activities of these two women demonstrated the generation and use of social capital. They had a shared understanding of the reasons for crop failure in the village and their beliefs that solutions should be sought from empirically based knowledge and that villagers could learn to be self-sustaining. They showed trust in each other, despite the lack of trust that others had for them, and they used this trust to build social institutions which attracted others. The new voluntary associations established sets of mutual expectations, recognised roles, and positively sanctioned behaviours. Thus, the network of women who formed Twegombe and the other associations greatly increased the social capital in their communities.

Both these women broke with the prevailing cultural orientations in their environment. These orientations favoured hierarchy as the way to organise productive relations and embeddedness as the way to define the relationship of the person to the group. The women's independent, innovative, and self-assertive behaviour, and the egalitarian manner in which they set up their association, directly opposed these taken-for-granted cultural values. Through their actions, they moved the culture of those who joined them toward greater intellectual autonomy and egalitarianism. This opened the zone of proximal development they created to influence from outside sources of knowledge and increased readiness to learn from empirically grounded experience rather than to persist in traditional ways. It also enabled them to evaluate ideas based on how well they worked rather than on who in the hierarchy proposed them.

Before arriving at appropriate ways to help villages to escape from poverty, researchers and policy makers need to study the zones of proximal development in the villages. Based on our experience analysing the zone of proximal development and the cultural learning in the Ugandan communities we studied, we suggest the following propositions as guides in carrying out this task. (Chapter 5, figure 5.1).

Proposition 1: In any zone of proximal development, there are points of normative consensus that set the boundaries for cultural learning.

For example, (a) describes the crucial normative consensus that prevented development in our focal community and (b) describes the alternative view that became the normative consensus in the rejuvenated zone of proximal development.

(a) Farming is very difficult and farming activities cannot provide enough food to feed yourself or your family. The soil is barren, the land is rocky and the rains come at the wrong time. So no matter how much you try, crop farming will never improve your situation.

(b) Farming is easy and interesting, if you know how to create manure from ordinary household refuse. If you learn to fertilise your soil by using home-made manure, crop farming on the plot you have will provide enough food to feed your family.

Proposition 2: Density and support mobilisation lead to interpersonal learning and to institutionalisation of norms and of values.

Example: The members of Twegombe who were mobilised spent their time together in intensive interaction aimed at learning methods of successful farming. This learning took place through direct interpersonal interaction of hands-on experience and observation rather than lectures. As they interacted, the women came to share and institutionalise norms about how to work together, how to farm, how to relate to their families and how to run their home finances. Crop farming and the reorganised modes of living it required took on positive value for them. Moreover, they came to value themselves more as worthy and competent people and to value cooperative activities among women.

Proposition 3: Interpersonal learning leads to intrapersonal or customised learning.

Example: Women from other villages observed Hajati Kalema and learned from her how she got maximum crop yields from her plot. But they did not then simply apply this knowledge unchanged to their own individual land. Rather, they internalised and customised it to fit their own circumstances such as smaller plots or different terrain. Moreover, they founded their own association and sought knowledge and skills relevant to their own circumstances from other experts.

Proposition 4: Intrapersonal or customised learning releases individual creativity and innovativeness that can create a new zone of proximal development.

Example: When people internalise and customise the knowledge and skills they have acquired, they come to understand not only how things happen but why. This deeper understanding enables them to change and innovate, to generate new ways of identifying and coping with problems. If they then make the effort to interest the community in the new skills, knowledge and perspectives they have developed, they can create a new or revitalised zone of proximal development.

The above propositions point to the focal issues that concern the social psychological approach to development we propose. These propositions make clear that the zone of proximal development is the key to whether behavioural poverty will persist in a community or whether it will move toward greater well-being. The propositions spell out the nature of zones of proximal development and the influences on them. The cases described in Chapters 5 and 7 concretely illustrate the elements that make up zones of proximal development. First, they are networks of interacting individuals. Second, these networks are the site of cultural (interpersonal) learning. Third, they encompass some degree of intellectual capital, some technological know-how and a set of shared understandings about the causes of events. These characteristics underline a major conclusion of this work: escaping from behavioural poverty and moving into well-being depends upon social interaction among community members and across community boundaries, rather than on the actions of individuals. The interaction can be between members of a community but because of the likelihood of the decay of the zone of proximal development this interaction should be as much between communities as within communities.

The three elements of zones of proximal development can guide researchers and planners to address particular sets of questions. Viewing the zones as networks raises questions about who the network members are, how dense the interaction in the network is, and what are the relevant individual behaviours that do or do not translate into community action. Viewing zones as learning networks raises the questions of what knowledge and skills network members have, how these are distributed among them, and how available they are for others to acquire. Viewing zones as repositories of intellectual capital, technological know-how and understandings about the causes of events raises another set of questions. What is the group as a whole capable of doing; should they come to share the knowledge and skills? What understandings regarding the nature and causes of the problems of poverty that they confront do they share or contest? And what sources of willingness to experiment with new ways of solving community problems are there, and what sources of resistance to innovation?

Studying the zone of proximal development in a community can provide such information about a target population. This, therefore, is where knowledge based-assistance should begin if behavioural poverty is to be eliminated.

Bibliography

Achebe, C. (1958). *Things Fall Apart.* Heinemann, African Writers Series.

Adler, P.S. and Kwon Seok-Woo (2002). Social Capital: Prospects for a New Concept. *Academy of Management Review.* 27 (1) 17-40.

Afonja, Simi and Aina, Bisi (1995). Introduction. *Nigerian Women in Social Change. The Programme in Women's Studies.* Ile-Ife, Obafemi Awolowo University Press,

Ahianzu, A. (1995). *Type A Method for Management Research in Africa: Enunciating a Culture-Specific Paradigm.* International Annual Management Conference on Competing in the 21st Century. Kampala, Makerere University Business School.

Akong'a J. (1995). *The growth-positive and growth-negative cultural characteristics in African societies.* Paper presented at a regional seminar on cultural dimensions to appropriate management in Africa. Makerere University.

Ali, Abdel Gadir Ali (1999). The Challenge of Poverty Reduction in Africa. *East African Social Science Review,* 15 (2) 79-105.

Alkire, S. (2001) *Valuable Freedoms: Putting Sen's Capability Approach to work in Poverty Reduction.* Oxford, Oxford University Press

Arrow, K.J. (2000). Observations on Social Capital. In Partha Dasgupta and Ismail, Serageldin. *Social Capital: A Multifaceted Perspective.* Washington: The World Bank.

Bandura, A. (1977). *Social Learning Theory.* Englewood Cliffs: N.J. Prentice Hall. Bandura, A. (1978). The Self-System in Reciprocal Determinism. *American Psychologist,*33, 344-358.

Blunt, P. (1983) *Organisational Theory and Behaviour: An African Perspective.* London: Longmans.

Bret, E.T. (1989). *Servicing Small Farmers under Duress: Institutional Crises and Reconstruction in Uganda.* Brighton, Sussex.

Bret, E.T. (1992) *Cost Effective Services for the Rural Poor: Policy and Institutional Reform in Uganda.* Brighton: Sussex.

Briggs, Xavier de Souza (1998). Brown Kids in White Suburbs: Housing Mobility and the Multiple Sources of Social Capital. *Housing Policy Debate* 1998 9 (1) 177-221.

Burt, R.S. (1997) The Contingent Value of Social Capital. *Administrative Science Quarterly,* 42, 339-365.

Canadian International Development Agency Involving Culture (1995). *A Fieldworker's Guide to Culturally Sensitive Development.* Paris: UNESCO.

Carasco, J., Munene, J.C., Kasente, D.H., and Odada, M. (1996). *Factors Influencing Effectiveness in Primary Schools. A Baseline Study.* Kampala: Uganda National Examination Board.

Cohen, J.M. and Uphoff, N. (1977). *Rural Development Participation. Concepts and Measures for Project Design, Implementation and Evaluation.* Ithaca: Rural Development Committee, Cornell University.

Cole, M.(1996).*Cultural Psychology: A Once and Future Discipline.* Cambridge: The Belknap Press of Harvard University Press.

Coleman, J.S. (1988). Social Capital in the Creation of Human Capital. *American Journal of Sociology* S95-S120

Community Development Resource Network (1997). Bundibugyo Action Aid Project.

Community Development Resource Network(1996). Dryland Farmers Resource Centre (Coopibal)

Cooksey, B. (1994). Who is Poor in Tanzania? A Review of Recent Poverty Research. In M.S.D. Bachwa, *Poverty Alleviation in Tanzania: Recent Research Issues.* Dar Es Salaam: Dar Es Salaam University Press.

Diagne, S.B. and Ossebi (1996). *The Cultural Question in Africa. Issues, Politics, and Research Prospect.* Senegal, CODESRIA.1996.

Douglas, M. (1982). *Risk and Blame. Essays in Cultural Theory.* London, Routledge.

European Commission, DG VIII. (1995). *Partners in Development-* EU and NGOs European Commission, Brussels.

Fallers, L.A. (1965). *Bantu Bureaucracy. A Century of Political Evolution Among the Basoga of Uganda.* Chicago: The University of Chicago Press.

Feather, N.T. (1994). Values and Culture. In Lonner, W.J. & Malpass, R. (Eds). *Psychology and culture* (pp. 183-189). New York: Allyn & Bacon.

Frese, M. (2000). *Success and failure of microbusiness owners in Africa. A Psychological Approach.* London: Quorum Books.

Frese, M. & Zapf, D. (1994). Actions as the core of work psychology: A German approach. In Triandis, H. C., Dunnette M. D. & Hough, J. M. (Eds.). *Handbook of Industrial and Organizational Psychology*, Vol. 4. (2nd Ed.). Palo Alto, CA: Consulting Psychology Press.

Frese, M., Fay, D., Hilburger, T., Leng, K. & Tag, A. (1997). The concept of personal initiative: Operationalization, reusability, and validity in two German samples. *Journal of Occupational and Organisational Psychology*, 70, 139 - 161.

Geertz, C. (1983). *Local Knowledge: Further Essays in Interpretive Anthropology.* New York: Basic Books.

Geertz, C. (1975). *The Interpretation of Cultures.* London: Hutchinson.

Gilbert, A. J. (1989). Things Fall Apart: Psychological Theory in Times of Rapid Social Change. *South African Journal of Psychology*, 19(2) 91-100.

Granovetter, M.S. (1985) Economic Action, Social Structure and Embeddedness. *American Journal of Sociology.* 91 481-510.

Granovetter, M.S. (1973). The Strength of Weak Ties, *American Journal of Sociology*, 78, 1360 - 1380.

Gyekye, K. (1987). *An Essay on African Philosophical thought: The Akan Conceptual Scheme.* Philadelphia: Temple University Press.

Harrison, P.(1982). *Inside the Third World.* London: Paladin Grafton Books.

Heider, F. (1958). *The Psychology of Interpersonal Behaviour.* Wiley, New Jersey.

Hofstede, G. (1991) *Cultures and Organisations: Software of the Mind.* London: McGraw Hill.

Hyden, G. (1983) No *Shortcuts to Progress: African Development Management in Perspective.* London: Heinemann.

Iguisi, O. (1995). *The Role of Culture in Appropriate Management.* Paper Presented at a Regional Seminar on Culture Dimensions and Appropriate and Effective Management in Africa. Makerere University Economic Policy Research Center.

Illfe, J. (1983). *The Emergence of African Capitalism.* London: Macmillan.

Jahoda, G. (1984). Do We Need a Concept of Culture? *Journal of Cross Cultural Psychology,* 15 139-152

Johnston R. & Lawrence, P.R. (1998). Beyond Vertical Integration – The Rise of the Value-Adding Partnership. In Thompson G., Frances J., Levacic, R. and Mitchell, J. *Markets, Hierarchies, and Networks. The Coordination of Social Life.* London: Sage Publications.

Kagitcibasi, C. (1997). Individualism and collectivism. In J. W. Berry, M. H. Segall and C. Kagitcibasi (Eds.), *Handbook of Cross-Cultural Psychology,* Vol. 3, 2nd Edition (pp. 1-50). Boston: Allyn & Bacon.

Kapferer, B. (1973). Social Networks and Conjugal Role. In Boissevain J. and Mitchell, J.C. (eds). *Network Analysis: Studies in Human Interaction.* The Hague: Mouton.

Keyes, C. L., Schwartz A. & Vidal, A.C.(1998). Networks and Nonprofits: Opportunities and Challenges in an Era of Federal Devolution. *Housing Policy Debate* 7, (2) 201-229.

Klitgaard, R.(1994). Taking Culture into Account From Let's to How. In I. Serageldin & J. Taboroff (eds), *Culture and Development in Africa.* Washington DC: World Bank.

Knoke D. & Kuklinski, J.H. (1998). Network Analysis: Basic Concepts. In G. Thompson G., J. Levacic & R. Michell (eds). *Markets, Hierarchies, and Networks. The Condition of Social Life.* London: Sage Publications.

Knowles (1970).

Korten, D. C. (1992). *Getting to the 21st Century: Voluntary Action and the Global Agenda.* Connecticut: Kumarian Press.

Marris, P. (1968). The Social Barriers to African Entrepreneurship. *Journal of Development Studies.* 5 (1) 29-38.

Matovu, N.D. (1995). *Gender Relations and the Effectiveness of the Heifer Project for Women Farmers in Mpigi District, Uganda.* MA Gender Studies. Makerere University Department of Women Studies, Faculty of Social Sciences.

Mbiti, J. (1969). *African Philosophy and Religion.* London, Longmans.

Miles, M.B. & Huberman, A.M. (1994). *Qualitative Data Analysis: An Expanded Source* Book. London: Sage Publications.

Ministry of Finance, Planning and Economic Development (MFPED) (2000). *Learning from the Poor: Uganda Participatory Assessment Report.* Kampala: The Republic of Uganda.

Ministry of Planning and Economic Development (1997). *Poverty Eradication Action Plan: A National Challenge for Uganda V 1*. Ministry of Planning and Economic Development

Munene, J.C. (1999). *Culture And Entrepreneurship: Talking Points. Entrepreneurship, Culture and Small Business Growth in Africa*: MUBS, 8-10.

Munene, J.C. (1995). Not-on-Seat: An Investigation of Some Correlates of Organisational Citizenship Behaviour in Nigeria. *Applied Psychology: An International Review* 44 (2), 111-122.

Munene, J.C. & Isingoma, E.(2002). The Cultural Interface And Cultural Value-Based Social Capital: Some Of The Cultural Values And Practices That Matter In Uganda. Eager: Equity And Growth Through Economic Research. Makerere Institute of Social Research.

Munene, J.C., Odada, M., Kasente, D., Carasco, J., Epeju, C., Obwoya, S., Omona, M. and Kinyera, G.A. (1997). *Teachers' Work Experience and Pupils' Schooling Experience as Determinants of Achievement in Primary Schools*. Kampala, Uganda National Examination Board.

Munene, J.C. Schwartz, S.H. & Smith, P.B.(2000). Development in Sub-Saharan Africa: Cultural Influences and Managers' Decision Behaviour. *Public Administration and Development,* 20, 339-351.

Nahapiet, J. & Ghoshal S. (1998). Social Capital, Intellectual Capital and the Organisational Advantage. *Academy of Management Review,* 23 (2), 242-266.

Namatovu, R. (2000). *Team, Networking and Performance in Village Banks*. MBA Dissertation. Makerere University Business School.

Narayan, D.(1997). *Voices of the Poor: Poverty and Social Capital in Tanzania.* Washington: The World Bank.

Nasfger, E. W. (1969). The Effect of the Nigerian Extended Family on Entrepreneurial Activity. *Economic Development and Cultural Change*. 18 25-33.

Noble, M. (1973). Social Network: its Use as a Conceptual Framework in Family Analysis. In Boissevain J. and Mitchell, J.C. (eds.). *Network Analysis: Studies in Human Interaction*. The Hague: Mouton.

Nsamenang, A.B. & Dawea, A. (1998). Developmental Psychology as Political Psychology in Sub-Saharan Africa: the Challenge of Africanisation. *Applied Psychology: An International Review*. 47

Okwi Okiira, P. and Kaija, Darlison (2000). The Distribution of Welfare in Uganda. *East African Social Science Review,* 16, 71-93.

Onwejeogwu, M.A. (1995). *Development in Africa: Common Cultural Values Central for Effective Managerial and Administrative Training Programmes.* Paper Presented at a Regional Seminar on Culture Dimensions and Appropriate and Effective Management in Africa. Makerere University

Organisation of African Unity (Undated) Cultural Charter for Africa.

Ostrom, E. (2000). Social Capital: A Fad or a Fundamental Concept? In P. Dasgupta & I. Serageldin. *Social Capital: A Multifaceted Perspective*. Washington: The World Bank.

Parrinder, G. (1962). *African Traditional Religion*. New York: Harper and Row.

Putnam, R. D. (1993). *Making Democracy Work: Civic Traditions in Modern Italy*. Princeton, New Jersey: Princeton University Press.

Paul, S. (1990). *Participation in Development Projects*. Washington: World Bank Press.

Poverty and Gender Inequality in Bundibugyo (1997). Bundibugyo Action Aid Project. Midterm Review.

Rotter, J.B. & Hochreich, D.J. (1975). *Personality*. Glenview, Ill.: Scot-Foreman.

Sagiv, L., & Schwartz, S. H. (2000). National cultures: Implications for organizational structure and behaviour. In N. N. Ashkanasy, C. Wilderom, & M. F. Peterson (Eds.), *The Handbook of Organizational Culture and Climate* (pp. 417-436). Newbury Park, CA: Sage.

Sandbrook, R. (1982). *The Politics of Basic Needs: urban Aspects of Assaulting Poverty in Africa*. London: Heinemann.

Savane, M (1983). Introduction to Another Development with Women. *Development Dialogue*, 1-2.

Schwartz, S. H. (1994a). Beyond Individualism/Collectivism: New cultural dimensions of values. *In Individualism and Collectivism: Theory, Method and Applications*, eds. U. Kim, H.C. Triandis, C. Kagitcibasi, S-C. Choi and G. Yoon, pp. 85-119. Sage, Newbury Park, CA.

Schwartz, S.H. (1994b). Are there universal aspects in the content and structure of values? *Journal of Social Issues,* 50, 19-45.

Schwartz, S.H. & Ros, M. (1995). Values in the West: A theoretical and empirical challenge to the Individualism-Collectivism cultural dimension. *World Psychology,* 1, 99-122.

Schwartz, S.H. (1997). Values and Culture. In D. Munro, S. Carr and J. Schumaker, *Motivation and Culture*, (69-84). London: Routledge.

Schwartz, S. H. (1997). Values and Culture. In D. Munro, S. Carr, & J. Schumaker (Eds.), *Motivation and Culture* (69-84). New York: Routledge.

Schwartz, S.H. (1992). Universals in the Structure and Content of Values: Theoretical Advances and empirical Tests in 20 Countries. In M.H. Zanna (Ed.). *Advances in Experimental Social Psychology* Orlando: Academic Press.

Schwartz, S.H. (1999). Cultural Value Differences: Some Implications for Work. *Applied Psychology: An International Review,* 48, 23-47.

Seibert, S.E., Kraimer, M.I. & Liden, R.C. (2001). A Social Capital theory of Career Success. *Academy of Management Journal,* 44 (2), 219-237.

Segall, M.H. (1984). More than we Need to Know about Culture, But we are Afraid not to Ask. *Journal of Cross Cultural Psychology*, 15, 153-162.

Sen, A. (1997). *On Economic Inequality*. Oxford, Clarendon Press.

Sen, G. & Crown, C. (1985). *Development, Crises and Alternative Visions: Third World Women's Perspective*. New Delhi: DAWN.

Snyder, M. (2000). *Women in African Economies: From the Burning Sun to Boardroom*. Kampala: Fountain Publishers.

Serageldin, I (1994). The Challenge of a Holistic Vision: Culture, Empowerment, and the Development Paradigm. In I. Serageldin & J. Taboroff (Eds.), *Culture and Development in Africa* (137-164). Washington D: World Bank.

Serageldin, I. & Grootaert, C. (2000). Defining Social Capital: An Integrating View. In P. Dasgupta and I. Serageldin (Eds.). *Social Capital: A Multifaceted Perspective*. Washington: The World Bank.

Serageldin I. & Taboroff J. (1994). *Culture and Development in Africa. Washington DC:* World Bank.

Shaw, M.E. &Costanzo, P.R. (1970). *Theories of Social Psychology*. New York: McGraw Hill

Solow, R.M.(2000). Notes on Social Capital and Economic Performance. In P. Dasgupta and I. *Social Capital: A Multifaceted Perspective*. Washington: The World Bank.

Ssekamwa, J.C. (1984). *A Sketch Map History of East Africa*. Kampala, T.& E. Publishers

Thompson, G. (1998). Introduction. In Thompson G., Frances J., Levacic, R. & Mitchell, J. *Markets, Hierarchies, and Networks. The Coordination of Social Life*. London: Sage Publications.

Trompenaars, F. & Hampden-Turner, C. (1998). *Riding the Waves of Culture. Understanding Cultural Diversity in Global Business*. New York: McGraw Hill.

Uganda IEQ Core Team (1999). *Perspectives of Quality Learning: From Research to Action*. Uganda Improving Education Quality Case Study. Ministry of Education and Sports. Improving Educational Quality Project.

Uganda Participatory Poverty Assessment Report (UPAP) (2000) *Learning from the Poor. Ministry of Finance, Planning and Economic Development*. The Republic of Uganda.

UNESCO (1982). *Mexico Declaration on Cultural Policies*. Article 16. Paris, UNESCO.

UNESCO (1995). *The Cultural Dimension of Development: Towards a Practical Approach*. Paris. UNESCO.

Uphoff, N. (2000). Understanding Social Capital: Learning from the Analysis and Experience of Participation. In P. Dasgupta and I. Serageldin. *Social Capital: A Multifaceted Perspective*. Washington: The World Bank.

Van Vlaenderen, H. S., & Nkwinti, G. (1993). Participatory Research as a tool for community development. *Development Southern Africa*, 10 (2), 211-228.

Vygotsky, L.S. (1978). *Mind in Society: The Development of Higher Mental Processes*. Cambridge, Mass.: Harvard University Press.

Wallace, T., Crowther, S., & Shepherd, A. (1996). *Standardizing Influences on UK NGO's Policies and Procedures*. Oxford: World View Publishing.

Wertsch, J.V. & Kanner, (1992). A Sociocultural Approach to Intellectual Development. In R.J. Stemberg & C A Berg (Eds.). *Intellectual Development* (328-349). New York: Cambridge University Press.

Wertsch, J.V. & Stone, C.A. (1985). The Concept of Internalisation in Vygotsky's Account of the Genesis of Higher Mental Functions. In J.V. Wertsch (Eds.), *Culture, Communication and Cognition: Vygotskian Perspective*. (Pp.162-182).Cambridge: Cambridge University Press.

Wertsch, J.V. (1997). *Vygotsky and the Social Formation of Mind*. Cambridge, Massachusetts, Harvard University Press.

Wildavsky A. (1994). How cultural theory can contribute to understanding and promoting Democracy, Science and Development. In I. Serageldin & J. Taboroff (Eds.) *Culture and Development in Africa.* Washington DC: World Bank.

Wilkinson, D. (1995). Central Civilisations. In S.K. Sanderson (ed), *Civilisations and World Systems. Studying World Historical Change.* (pp 46-74). London, Altamira Press.

Willis. G. (1994). Networking and Its Leadership Processes. *Leadership and Organisational DevelopmentJournal,*15, 0143-7739.

Woolcock, M. & Narayan, D. (2000). 'Social capital: implications for development theory, research, and policy'.*World Bank Research Observer,* 15(2), 225-49.

Index